Eisenhower

Eisenhower

Martin Blumenson

Editor-in-Chief: Barrie Pitt
Editor: David Mason
Art Director: Sarah Kingham
Picture Editor: Robert Hunt
Consultant Art Editor: Denis Piper
Designer: John Watson
Illustration: John Batchelor
Photographic Research: Carina Dvořak
Cartographer: Richard Natkiel

First published in the United States 1972
This Pan/Ballantine edition published 1973 by Pan Books Ltd,
33 Tothill Street, London SW1

Printed Offset Litho in Great Britain
by Cox & Wyman Ltd, London, Fakenham and Reading

Contents

He made it work.

Introduction by Barrie Pitt

When two or more nations join together to fight a common foe, it is not sufficient merely that they have a common interest for the venture to have any hope of success. National characteristics and national pride, to say nothing of national interests, play their part in making the course of allied cooperation a difficult one, but in the end all three of these very natural traits must be subordinated to the pursuit of the corporate aim. It is easy to agree upon the ideal; this is usually the first, and in too many cases the only, point upon which would-be collaborators see eye to eye. It is far more difficult to reach agreement on method, and a study of military history shows that complete unanimity between multi-racial forces is rarely achieved. Success in fact is most likely to result when allies are able to operate independently of one another but to their mutual advantage.

Modern warfare is too complex for these circumstances to occur often; battles must be run to strict time-tables, coordination between units must be effective and, more important, overall command must be exercised by someone whose orders will be obeyed and who can if necessary vary the planned operation in accordance with the exigencies of the moment.

When America entered the war in 1941, her rulers immediately faced a vital decision as to which theatre should be given first priority, for it was manifestly impossible, even for a country with America's huge resources, to achieve the same concentration of men and material in both European and Pacific areas. With the decision made in favour of the European theatre, it was only natural that from the outset General George C Marshall, the United States Army Chief of Staff, should press for the opening of a 'second-front' against Germany. At once this caused dissention, for the British refused point blank to consider an attack across the English Channel at that point in time, feeling with some justification that premature action would result in disastrous failure.

But despite their contention that 1942 was too early to consider the reconquest of Europe, the British did recognise the necessity of mounting some sort of major offensive in order to help relieve pressure on the Russians. Stalin was bluntly outspoken in demanding action from his British and American allies and made it abundantly clear that he wanted it quickly. Thus was Operation 'Torch' conceived – the invasion of North Africa.

Because of French antipathy to the British – a mixture of resentment over the evacuation of the BEF from France, anger at the attacks carried out by the British on French warships in Dakar and Mers el Kebir to prevent them falling into German hands, and an historic, almost traditional, Anglophobia – it was considered politic to give the invasion force an American look. The political situation in North Africa was a delicate one and it was hoped that if the French could be persuaded to co-operate, the landings might go ahead with little loss of life; furthermore, it might be possible to induce the French to throw in their lot with the Americans and British and to join with them in attacking Rommel from the west.

The problems which would face the commander of Operation Torch would therefore be multifarious and difficult; he must step gently so as not to provoke the French, he must promote harmony between the British, who had been at war for three years, and his inexperienced American troops, and he must fight a military campaign against an experienced and redoubtable foe. On 25th July 1942, the Combined Chiefs of Staff appointed General Dwight D Eisenhower to command the Torch invasion with the title 'Commander-in-Chief, Allied Force'.

Dwight Eisenhower was a graduate of the Military Academy of West Point, an honours graduate of the Staff College, and he had served with distinction under such demanding and critical masters as Douglas MacArthur and George Marshall. His had been a brilliant career under peacetime conditions; he now faced the final proof in the acid test of war.

In the event, Eisenhower remained in the Mediterranean theatre until his appointment to command Operation 'Overlord' – the Normandy landings – during which time the Germans had been driven out of North Africa, Pantelleria and its neighbouring islands had been taken, Sicily had fallen, and the invasion of Italy begun. In addition to his military responsibilities in all these operations, he had not only been involved in the political negotiations in North Africa, but also in the haggling which pre-ceded the Italian surrender; now he undertook command of the greatest combined operation of all time, which, if successful, would be followed by a land campaign which must be continued until Germany surrendered unconditionally.

In this book, Martin Blumenson follows Eisenhower's career as Supreme Commander and examines the criticisms which have been levelled at his conduct of the war; the result is a well-balanced account depicting a man who cheerfully carried the huge responsibilities which were placed upon him. That Eisenhower was a 'lucky' commander is readily conceded, but 'luck' only put the finishing touches on his success; nothing within his power to control did he leave to chance – the risks he took were carefully calculated and there is ample proof that he was quite ready to shoulder the complete blame for any failure in the enterprises he undertook.

Probably no previous war has been followed by such a plethora of 'war books' as the Second World War. Never before have military commanders been so ruthlessly analysed by those with the benefit of hindsight, or by fellow participants who spent their time between armistice and publication date justifying their own actions. How often is it forgotten by those writing many years after the event and with access to both Allied and Axis documents, that commanders in the field have to make daily decisions based on what intelligence is provided from available sources – including enemy ones with a vested interest in deceit?

In the final analysis, much of the postwar criticism of the military commanders – on both sides – appears petty and carping against the historical fact of positive achievement. And few people would deny that Eisenhower, by whatever means and in spite of whatever theoretical shortcomings, achieved much.

Appointment

Early 1942 ; Dwight D Eisenhower when in charge of Operations Section, War Department General Staff, immediately prior to becoming Allied supreme commander

The story of Dwight D Eisenhower as Supreme Allied Commander in the Second World War turns about a central question asked by everyone, including himself, at every stage of his career: would he measure up to, was he capable of meeting successfully, the progressively larger challenges that confronted him?

From the summer of 1942, when he first became an Allied supreme commander, to the summer of 1945, when the European phase of the global war terminated, Eisenhower faced a series of increasingly complex situations. In command of a growing number of ground, sea, and air forces of the major Allies, the United States and Great Britain, plus military forces of France, Belgium, Czechoslovakia, Canada, Poland, New Zealand, South Africa, Australia, and other nations, he directed a coalition effort that was unique in the history of warfare. Responsible for the military operations of these forces, he was also involved in a host of political and administrative problems that were an inescapable part of waging war on so massive a scale.

That he mastered his difficulties was due in no small part to his own development as a leader, manager, and director. As his tasks broadened, so did his experience, and his capacities reflected, finally, the mature poise of a seasoned campaigner. Underneath the mild-mannered, likeable personality, the man with the smile, was a soldier made of steel.

His success depended in large measure upon his subordinates. He chose them – Bradley, Patton, Bedell Smith among the Americans – and they performed exceptionally well for him. He approved the selection of his Allied subordinate commanders, and they too – Alexander, Cunningham, Tedder, and others – were up to their tasks.

To a large extent, Eisenhower succeeded because of the unwavering support he received from his superiors. They allowed him to prove himself.

The political leaders of the United States and Great Britain, President Franklin D Roosevelt and Prime Minister Winston S Churchill, directed the war. In their military decisions they were assisted by the Combined Chiefs of Staff, which consisted of the British Chiefs of Staff and the American Joint Chiefs of Staff meeting together. George C Marshall, the US Army Chief of Staff, and Sir Alan Brooke, the Chief of the Imperial General Staff, were the most prominent members of this august body.

The Combined Chiefs planned the global strategy, allocated and distributed the available human and material resources to the fighting fronts, and coordinated the operations in the far-flung theaters throughout the world. They sent instructions to the supreme Allied commanders who were immediately under them and who were responsible for prosecuting the war in their particular theaters of operation.

Eisenhower first learned of his selection to be a supreme Allied commander at Claridge's Hotel in London. It was the evening of 25th July 1942, and the Second World War was nearing the end of its third year.

While Hitler's forces overran Poland in September, 1939, then divided it with Stalin, Britain sent an army to France. During the subsequent Phoney War, British, Belgian, and French forces remained inactive. In May 1940, the German blitzkrieg smashed the Allies in France. The British evacuated most of their troops at Dunkerque, and Belgium and France surrendered.

The battle of Britain in the summer and fall of 1940 averted a German invasion of England and closed with a precarious British victory. Hitler then moved to the east. He invaded the USSR in mid-1941, struck toward Moscow, but failed to reach the Russian capital before the onset of winter. In 1942, having conquered the rich agricultural lands of the Ukraine, Hitler sent his armies to the south, towards the oilfields of the Caucasus

Above: The four-star general at a London press conference with a selection of his subordinates
Below: Tent inspection by the Commanding General, European Theater

Above : The swastika flies for a short time in Stalingrad
Below : Erwin Rommel leads his men into Egypt in 1942. Germany seems invincible

Mark Clark, Eisenhower's assistant
in the task of organizing US forces in
Britain

and the industrial wealth of the Urals.
That drive would end at Stalingrad.

Meanwhile, Mussolini had brought
Italy into the war, and with German
help, Italian forces were engaged in
the Balkans and in North Africa. In
Libya and Egypt, British and Italo-
German forces fought a see-saw cam-
paign, with first one, then the other
holding the advantage. In the summer
of 1942, an Axis army under Erwin
Rommel was inside Egypt, at El
Alamein, a scant sixty miles from
Alexandria and the Nile.

The United States, bombed and
blasted into the Second World War by
the Japanese attack at Pearl Harbor,
was on the defensive in the Pacific
and was searching for a way to carry
out its Europe-first strategy, that is,
to devote the main American power
against the European foes and try to
knock them out before moving whole-
heartedly against Japan. In the summer of 1942, American military units
had yet to meet the European Axis
forces in battle.

Through discussions in the Combined Chiefs of Staff, British and
Americans were trying to hammer
out a mutually acceptable strategic
blueprint. They were endeavoring to
determine the best method of coming
to grips with the Axis forces. They
had already agreed that the best way
of grappling with the enemy was to
mount a cross-Channel attack from
England, invade the continent, engage
and defeat the major German forces,
and drive toward Berlin.

To this end, the Americans, with
British approval, initiated a massive
buildup of troops, weapons, equipment, and supplies in the United
Kingdom. When this force was ready,
it would, together with British,
Canadian, and other units also in
training, cross the Channel and liberate western Europe.

In charge of the American buildup
was Eisenhower, who arrived in
London on 24th June 1942. As the
Commanding General of the European
Theater of Operation, US Army
(ETOUSA), he was directly sub-
ordinate to the US Army Chief of
Staff, Marshall. With the assistance of
Mark W Clark, who commanded the
American ground troops in the United
Kingdom, Eisenhower had the job of
creating an American fighting force
and preparing it for combat.

Although the Allied partners had
agreed on a European strategy, they
were at odds on the issue of timing.
When should the Allies launch their
cross-Channel attack?

The Americans wished to invade the
continent in 1942 if possible, in 1943
at the latest. Highly conscious of the
demands of the war in the Pacific, they
hoped to win in Europe quickly. Given
their virtually unlimited resources,
the American strategists, particularly
Marshall, advocated what was called
a power thrust, a direct strike across
the Channel and an immediate drive
into Germany.

The British, lacking the industrial
base of the United States and already
fatigued by their wartime exertions,
were far more wary. Aware by experience of the strength of the Axis
forces and consequently cautious,
they felt that a cross-Channel invasion in 1942 would be premature,

Situation in Europe, 7th November 1942, on the eve of TORCH

and they refused to participate in an attack until success could be unconditionally guaranteed. They wanted no suicide landings, no more Dunkerque-type evacuations from a continental beachhead.

In this impasse, the political and military leaders of both nations came under severe pressure from the news media. Reflecting public opinion and shaping it too, newspapers and magazines in Britain and the United States urged loudly the necessity for a 'second front'. The Russians were taking the German onslaught for the second year, and unless the western Allies drew off some German units by opening their own theater of operations, the Russians might well succumb to the German fury.

The Americans, again personified by Marshall, saw the need of a land front in Europe to keep Russia in the war, and a cross-Channel endeavor seemed the most appropriate operation. The British, although understanding the necessity of keeping Russia in the war, were more interested in making Egypt secure. To them, the Middle East had overriding importance, for they wished to keep open the Gibraltar-Suez route to India.

In mid-July, Roosevelt sent Marshall and several high-ranking

British troops training in Scotland under the eye of Winston Churchill. His counter-proposal to an early invasion of Europe – landings in North Africa – was adopted

officials to London to reach agreement with the British on some offensive operations that could be undertaken in 1942. If Marshall could not persuade the British to do the cross-Channel invasion together with the Americans, he was to come up with an alternative that could be launched that year.

During the ensuing discussions, the British refused to prepare a Channel invasion until a more propitious time. As an alternative, Churchill suggested landings in French North-West Africa. The objective would be to land in French Morocco, Algeria, and Tunisia, and thereby threaten the rear of Rommel's forces in Libya and Egypt.

Marshall was certain that opening any other front would adversely affect the cross-Channel buildup. It would,

he was sure, drain resources away from the United Kingdom and make impossible an invasion of Europe even in 1943.

Yet Roosevelt's instructions were clear, and Marshall, with some reluctance and much misgiving, agreed to an invasion of French North-West Africa, which was codenamed TORCH.

American and British military and political leaders conferring together in London late in July decided to put an American in command of TORCH, for they wished to give the invasion forces an American look. The French had hostile feelings toward their former allies, the British, not only because they felt that the British had prematurely abandoned them in 1940, but also because they resented the British attacks on the French warships at Mers-el-Kebir and Dakar after the French surrender – the British had feared that the considerable French fleet might fall into German hands.

Although the French were sure to resist a British invasion, they might be more friendly toward the Americans, their traditional allies. Perhaps the Americans could get ashore with little or no fighting, and then the French, who certainly hated the British less than they did the Germans, might join the Allies and march on Rommel's rear.

The upshot of a meeting on 25th July was the decision to place Eisenhower in charge of the North African invasion. The Combined Chiefs also left him at the head of the cross-Channel buildup. The theory was that he could best shift resources from one undertaking to the other.

There was also some doubt that he was capable of commanding the first Anglo-American combat venture in the European theater. For that reason, instead of being named Supreme Allied Commander, he was called Commander-in-Chief, Allied Force. The distinction was subtle, but it reflected the idea, present in some quarters, that Marshall might return

Strand von Dieppe! 19.8.4_

from Washington and lead the American and British troops ashore.

After the meeting ended, Marshall went back to his suite at Claridge's. He asked Eisenhower to come and see him. When Eisenhower arrived, he learned that he was to take charge of the amphibious operation designed to invade French North-West Africa.

Who was this young and inexperienced officer who was to assume a burden that was as unexpected as it was complicated? As the Dieppe raid, an Anglo-Canadian venture across the Channel, would clearly show the following month, an amphibious operation was the most difficult and delicate expedition that military forces could possibly undertake. Loading vessels with troops according to predetermined schedules and in the strength necessary to overcome resistance on the shore, furnishing naval and air protection, and finally, after transporting the amphibious forces across the ocean, putting them

Lessons for the Allies : abandoned tanks and burning landing craft at Dieppe

ashore with a reasonable chance of succeeding – these were all extremely hazardous and intricate problems. They demanded meticulous planning and highly competent execution. Furthermore, there was no prior experience on which to build this Anglo-American expedition. There were not even enough ships to carry the troops to North Africa.

It was asking a great deal of any man to assume these awesome responsibilities. But to ask a man to assume these duties who had never led soldiers in combat before appeared to be asking the impossible. Could Eisenhower measure up to the pressures of the overall task?

Originally a farm boy from Kansas, representing the virtues of a rural environment, he was now fifty-two years old. He was a graduate of the Military Academy at West Point, an honors graduate of the Command and

15

Cadet Eisenhower at West Point in 1915

General Staff College at Fort Leavenworth, where he stood first in a class of 245 students, and a graduate of the Army War College.

His formal military education was complete, yet his experience seemed to be less than adequate. During the First World War, he had remained in the United States as a commander and trainer of tankers. Since then he had had a variety of assignments, including a tour of duty as Assistant to Douglas MacArthur, who had been Military Advisor to the Commonwealth of the Philippine Islands. Eisenhower had attracted favorable notice in 1940 and 1941 as a staff officer during large-scale maneuvers held in the United States. But he had had no real test in battle.

His rise in rank – and it would be a meteoric rise – really started in February 1942, when Marshall appointed him Chief of the War Plans Division of the War Department General Staff. This was Marshall's own command post to help him control and coordinate the American contributions to the global struggle.

A ceremonial occasion in Manila during his tour of duty under Douglas MacArthur, 1935

Later it would be known as the Operations Division, Office of the Chief of Staff.

As head of a small group of planners, Eisenhower worked closely with Marshall. In a very short time he demonstrated what were probably his outstanding qualities – his intelligence, his adaptability, and his capacity to assume and discharge responsibility.

Having impressed Marshall, he was sent to London in June to command ETOUSA. He had hardly embarked on this job, he had hardly proved his capacities, particularly to the British, when he received the TORCH assignment.

Many observers believed that his background was inadequate for a man

now designated to lead a coalition effort involving army, navy, and air force elements of the two major Allied partners.

Thus it was with some concern that the Combined Chiefs of Staff confided to Eisenhower the direction of the first Allied assault that would, hope-

Third Army maneuvers in 1941 ; Eisenhower with General Walter Krueger. His inexperience in battle was later held against him by his critics

fully, start the momentum that would take the Allies down the road to victory in Europe.

'Torch'

The landings near Algiers;
fortunately losses were light

The first requirement for TORCH was an Allied command structure, and Eisenhower immediately set about to form one. Mainly in order to maintain the pretense that the invasion was American, he named Clark to be his deputy commander. As Clark took charge of the immense task of planning for the landings, Eisenhower assembled his Allied Force Headquarters (AFHQ), an organization that would aid him in the multifarious tasks of commanding the operation.

He decided to follow the precepts of the American staff system rather than those of the British, who had a slightly different method of operating. Walter Bedell Smith would come to London from Washington in September to be his Chief of Staff, and Smith would

preside over the heads of the various staff sections, the G-1 (Personnel), G-2 (Intelligence), G-3 (Operations), and G-4 (Logistics), plus others, for example, Medical, Ordnance, Signal, and the like.

Although this conformed with American practice, Eisenhower modified it in order to obtain an integrated Anglo-American staff, that is, a balanced representation of British and American staff officers. Since it was difficult to establish a single administrative and logistical service for both nations, the G-1 and G-4 functions were fulfilled in parallel fashion, with Americans looking after American personnel and supplies, and British officers handling the same for the British forces. Eisenhower named a British officer as his G-2, then appointed an American to serve as the deputy G-2. He had an American officer as his G-3, with a British officer assigned as the G-3 deputy.

AFHQ thus became a balanced collection of British and American officers working closely together to achieve the common aims of the alliance.

There were, of course, inevitable difficulties. Although British and Americans spoke much the same language, they sometimes used different words for the same meaning, and their slang was not the same. There were obvious differences in national temperament, attitudes, and outlook. The traditions and customs of both nations were dissimilar. There were, thus, opportunities for friction and misunderstanding.

Eisenhower insisted that the coalition would work only if AFHQ operated as an integrated and unified team. Obsessed with this requirement, Eisenhower once sent an American home in disgrace when he learned that this American staff officer had called his British counterpart a British SOB; calling him simply a SOB would have been all right.

As a consequence of Eisenhower's insistence and personal example,

19

Walter Bedell Smith, brought to London from Washington to be Eisenhower's Chief of Staff for TORCH

James H Doolittle, heading Western Air Command

AFHQ became a close-knit organization, where the differences between the two nationalities were the insignificant ones of accent and uniform. British officers had a coffee break with their American colleagues every morning; American officers had tea with their British associates every afternoon. Although these may have been trivial manifestations of a coalition solidarity, they represented a deeper commitment by the individuals of both nations to a single minded devotion to the common war aims.

With Eisenhower at the apex of the coalition command system for TORCH and with AFHQ formed to help him run the show, Eisenhower built his subordinate command structure. All the commanders immediately under him would report directly to him. Eisenhower would have ultimate authority to do whatever had to be done, and he would take ultimate responsibility for whatever success or failure resulted.

In command of the Allied naval forces was Sir Andrew B Cunningham. Sir William L Welsh headed the Eastern Air Command, composed of Royal Air Force units, while James H Doolittle headed the Western Air Command, composed of US Army Air Forces; later, Sir Arthur W Tedder would command both under the banner of the Allied Air Forces in the Mediterranean, thereby coordinating under Eisenhower's direction both British and American air operations.

Commanding the army or ground forces was Sir Kenneth Anderson, who would head the British First Army and who would control the contingents making the amphibious assaults. There would be three landings, and therefore three task forces, all commanded by Americans in order to promote the American character of the initial invasion. George S Patton, Jr would command one task force sailing directly from the United States to land near Casablanca, French Morocco. Two task forces were to sail from the United Kingdom, one headed by Lloyd R Fredendall, who was scheduled to come ashore near Oran, the other by Charles W Ryder, to land near Algiers.

If the organizational and logistical matters connected with mounting and launching an invasion were formid-

Allied naval forces commander Admiral Sir Andrew Brown Cunningham (*front right*), with Alexander and Tedder. Beddell Smith is second from left in back row

able, the political implications of the landings were awesome. Spanish Morocco was deemed a sensitive point because of Franco's sympathy for Hitler; should Franco join the Axis and take an active part in the war, he might close the straits of Gibraltar to British shipping and perhaps even attack and interfere with the Allied forces trying to invade North Africa. Libya, an Italian possession, was the main base of supplies for Rommel's Army, which was quiet for the moment in Egypt.

But it was the problem of French North-West Africa itself that posed the most troublesome difficulties. French Morocco, Algeria, and Tunisia were neutral. After the French surrender in 1940, the German Armistice Commission permitted the French to maintain a standing army of 120,000 men equipped with obsolescent weapons; they were stationed in these colonies for the purpose of keeping the natives pacified. Hitler promised not to interfere with the administration

Patton commands the task force sailing direct from the US

of the French possessions, and the French promised to resist any attempt on the part of the Allies to invade.

The French were therefore committed to oppose the landings.

The planned TORCH invasion had as its aim the elimination of all the Axis forces from all of North Africa. The main Axis forces were in Libya and under Rommel in Egypt. But Libya and Egypt were too distant from the United States and Great Britain for the Allies to contemplate an immediate assault there from the sea. Even Tunisia was deemed too far and too dangerous, for the sensitive point of Spanish Morocco, together with the close proximity of Sardinia, Sicily, and southern Italy to Tunisia, posed complications. The Allies felt that it would be an unwarranted risk to land at once in Tunisia because the Germans and Italians were relatively close to Tunisia and could pour troops into that area.

Thus, the Allies would land in Morocco, mainly to guarantee the sea lanes directly to the United States; and in Algeria. From Algeria, they would try to move speedily eastward into Tunisia and thereby threaten Rommel in Libya.

If the French permitted the Anglo-Americans to come ashore without fighting, and if they resisted a German and Italian incursion into Tunisia, they would give the Allies enough time to move into Tunisia and counter an Axis build-up. Yet active and open French sympathy for the Allies and opposition against the Axis would break the Armistice agreement. Hitler, who was occupying half of metropolitan France, would certainly overrun the unoccupied part and put all of France under German control.

Because the French government at Vichy was watched closely by the Germans, there was no way for the

The leader of the Free French government in England visits North Africa. Charles de Gaulle at Tunis Airport in 1943

Allies to take Pétain into their confidence and disclose their landing plans. Most French colonial administrators in North Africa were loyal to Vichy, but their commitment to this Fascist-orientated government was less than wholehearted.

Convinced that they needed a man around whom the French colonial Army in North Africa could rally, the Allies searched for a figure of this sort. Charles de Gaulle, who had formed a Free French government in England and who refused to accept the validity of the Franco-German armistice, seemed to have the necessary qualities, but Roosevelt had a personal antipathy toward him; and besides, the French who were loyal to the legal government of France under Pétain regarded De Gaulle as a traitor.

Robert Murphy, a State Department official in North Africa, was in touch with Henri Giraud, a general who had escaped from a German prisoner of war camp (as he had during the First World War), who was a hero to Frenchmen, who had no political ties, and who was living in unoccupied France. Would Giraud, Murphy asked, come secretely to Gibraltar, where Eisenhower would establish his command

Henri Giraud, selected to ensure the cooperation of the French colonial army, with Eisenhower in Algeria

post, and consider bringing the French military forces in North Africa into the Allied side?

Giraud agreed, made rendezvous with an Allied submarine, and came to Gibraltar several days before the scheduled landings.

In London, Eisenhower was trying to fashion his insufficient resources – there were shortages in naval support and air cover, as well as in ground forces – into a viable amphibious operation. He and his staff worked hectically to prepare for the invasion that would take place on 8th November.

In mid-October, Eisenhower sent Clark to North Africa to confer secretly with French officials who were known to be sympathetic to the Allied cause. Clark travelled by submarine, came ashore, met his contacts, and was almost captured by the police. Yet he learned the exact details regarding the locations of French troops and guns at Oran and Algiers. He also impressed on the French the importance of preventing the Germans

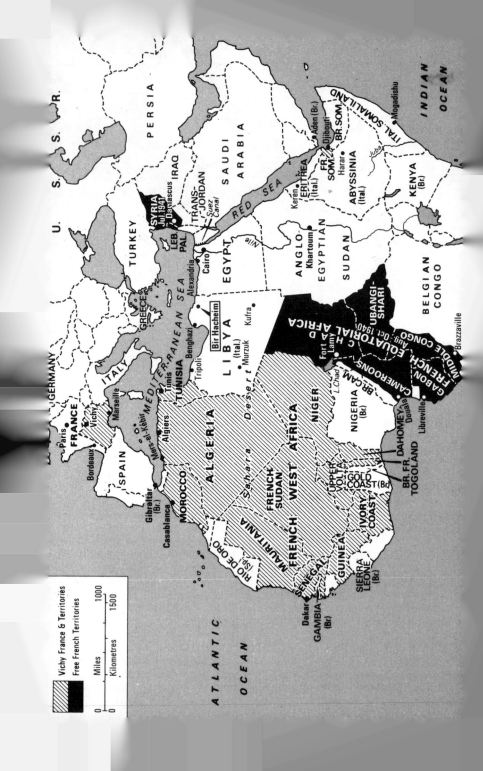

from entering Tunisia from Sicily and southern Italy.

Although there was no direct connection between Eisenhower's Allied forces preparing for TORCH and the British forces in Egypt facing Rommel's Italo-German army, the British attacked at El Alamein on 23rd October. General Alexander, who commanded the British Middle East theatre, and General Montgomery, who under Alexander commanded the British Eighth Army, defeated Rommel's troops and compelled him to withdraw from Egypt. Pursuing Rommel, they made him start a retreat across the 1,500-mile breadth of Libya, all the while searching for a defensive line on which to halt his withdrawal and stabilize the front.

If Montgomery pursued Rommel closely and kept him in flight, thereby pushing the Axis forces into the Mareth Line along the Libya-Tunisia border, and if Eisenhower's Allied landings succeeded and the troops could rush east toward Tunisia,

British troops thrust Rommel out of Egypt – toward the Allied landings in the west

Rommel would be trapped.

Early in November, Eisenhower flew to Gibraltar and set up his headquarters. In subterranean passages tunneled into the Rock, where walls were damp and light was dim – 'the most dismal setting we occupied during the war', Eisenhower later said – he awaited word on the progress of the invasion fleets steaming toward their landing areas, on the results of the air operations that were part of the scheme, and finally on the outcome of the efforts of the ground troops to get ashore.

Eisenhower also met with Giraud. He wanted the Frenchman to broadcast a statement to his countrymen in Morocco and Algeria, assuring them that the moment had arrived for them to throw off the German yoke and join their Allied brothers.

Giraud refused. He wanted to be the supreme commander of the invasion

forces, and he wished further – an impossibility from a technical point of view – to turn these forces in transit and send them into an invasion of southern France.

Despite Giraud's lack of realism, Eisenhower promised him command of some Allied forces once they were established in Algeria. Giraud could command those units guaranteeing the lines of supply leading to Tunisia, but only after the Allied troops were ashore and on their way to forestall an Axis intervention in Tunisia. Eisenhower also offered Giraud the civil administration of North Africa and funds to rebuild a French army and air force.

Giraud insisted on having the supreme command at once. Otherwise,

he threatened, the French would fight and repel the Allied landings.

On 8th November, despite the brave but futile resistance of French defenders, more than 100,000 American and British soldiers landed on the shores of French North-West Africa. The French officials who were sympathetic to the Allies were incapable of carrying out their self-assigned duties, and a comedy of errors was about to prolong the combat between the French and the Allied troops.

Fortunately, Admiral Darlan, Pétain's deputy, was in Algiers. His presence was a stroke of luck. He had gone to visit his son, stricken with polio, in a hospital. Commander-in-Chief of the French armed forces and thus the legal head of the military

The landings in Oran by a combined British and American convoy

establishment in North Africa, Darlan had the authority to stop the French opposition. Unlike Giraud, who was politically naive, Darlan was a shrewd politician.

On 9th November, Eisenhower sent Clark to Algiers to offer Darlan what he had earlier proposed to Giraud. Clark put enormous pressure on Darlan, and despite Pétain's insistence that the armistice of 1940 be honored and the invaders repulsed, Darlan ordered a cease-fire.

Meanwhile, German and Italian planes were landing troops in Bizerte and Tunis and establishing a bridgehead in Tunisia. The French there took no action against them.

On 11th November, as Darlan took sole authority in French North-West Africa and called a halt to the French resistance against the Allies, Hitler's forces overran all of metropolitan France.

With Darlan now guaranteeing the security of the Allied forces in Morocco and Algeria, Eisenhower turned his eastermost forces from Algeria towards Tunisia. He also directed that the floating reserve of the Eastern Task Force, part of the British 78th Division, be sent ashore at Bougie, about a hundred miles east of Algiers, in order to be closer to the ultimate objective, the port of Tunis.

Coming to Algiers himself on 13th November, Eisenhower met with

Pétain's deputy, Admiral Darlan (center), flanked by Eisenhower and Major-General Clark, during the cease-fire negotiations

Darlan and ratified formally the deal that Clark and Murphy had made with the Frenchman. Eisenhower pledged to respect the continued control of the French over the administration of North Africa, to furnish food to the population, and to rearm the French military forces so they could join the Allies in the war against the Axis. In return, Darlan promised to keep the French fleet in Toulon and Dakar from falling into German hands, to support the Allied drive into Tunisia, and to keep order among the Arabs and thereby secure the lines of communication leading into Tunisia.

On that day Darlan took the title of High Commissioner and assumed responsibility for the civil powers in French North Africa. Giraud became Commander-in-Chief of the French military forces.

How difficult it was to secure these arrangements which were mutually beneficial and which appeared so simple was revealed in a letter that Eisenhower wrote to Bedell Smith:

'Every effort to secure organized and effective French cooperation runs into a maze of political and personal intrigue and the definite impression exists that . . . [no one] really wants to fight nor to cooperate whole-heartedly.' Without French help to guard the railways and roads and to keep the Arabs quiet, the Allies would have 'a tremendous job on our hands in this sprawling country'.

This was the Darlan deal, which received such widespread adverse publicity in Britain and the United States. Darlan was regarded as a German collaborator, a Fascist, and an enemy. How could Eisenhower have made an agreement with the enemies against whom the Allies were fighting? To work with Darlan seemed to destroy the idealistic language of the Atlantic Charter, the Four Freedoms that Churchill and Roosevelt had announced as their war aims, goals that made the Allied prosecution of the war a crusade against the evil for which the Axis stood.

What motivated Eisenhower was military necessity. His forces were unable to occupy all of French Northwest Africa and at the same time expel the Axis forces from Tunisia.

Darlan, Cunningham, Eisenhower and Giraud at a ceremony honoring the Unknown Soldier

'[I] can well understand some bewilderment in London and Washington with the turn that negotiations with French North Africans have taken,' Eisenhower wired the Combined Chiefs of Staff. 'The actual state of existing sentiment here does not . . . agree even remotely with some of [our] prior calculations . . . it is extremely important that no . . . precipitate action at home upset such equilibrium as we have been able to establish . . . I am certain that anyone who is not . . . on the ground can have no clear appreciation of the complex currents of feeling and of prejudice that influence the situation.'

The political turmoil in the United States and Britain that arose in the train of the Darlan deal and the questioning of his military policy wore down Eisenhower, who felt immense strain. About 1,800 American troops had been lost during the three days of the actual assault landings, whereas planning figures had estimated casualties at 18,000 – ten times as many. The Darlan deal had, at least theoretically, saved American lives by stopping the fighting.

'I regret that I must use so much of my own time to keep explaining these matters,' Eisenhower said. What irritated him was the widespread feeling that he was a nice guy, a naive soldier who had been taken in by a shrewd politician like Darlan.

After a week of torment, Eisenhower was able to emerge from the sole responsibility for the Darlan agreements. He forced his superiors to approve them. He sent the original Clark-Darlan document, which gave the Allies military rights while keeping the Vichy French in power, to the Combined Chiefs, who turned it over to Churchill and Roosevelt. With some uneasiness, the political leaders concurred in Eisenhower's arrangements.

The unfortunate result of the deal with Darlan was the continuation of Axis policies in French North-West Africa. Vichy-appointed officials remained in office. Underprivileged natives continued to have no political rights and few civil rights. Jews were persecuted as before. Political prisoners stayed in jails and concentration camps. Fascist gangs roamed the streets intimidating the population.

In the end, Eisenhower's policy failed to save the French warships at Toulon. On 25th November, as Germans prepared to board the vessels in the harbour, the French crews scuttled and sank three battleships, seven cruisers, and 167 other craft.

It could be said that Eisenhower had paid a high price for a minor gain. Darlan had kept North Africa quiet, but the French fleet was at the bottom of the sea. By the time Darlan had ordered a cease-fire in Algiers, Casablanca, and Oran, French soldiers had satisfied the demands of honour and were ready to quit. Perhaps Eisenhower's promises had been more important than Darlan's orders in bringing the French over to the Allied side.

Still, Eisenhower was unable to see what he might have done differently. He lacked enough troops to occupy North Africa without assistance. He was unable to work with De Gaulle's Free French. And he could have no confidence in Giraud, who was naive and rigid.

He had, in fact, succeeded in his first assignment as Supreme Allied Commander. TORCH had gained Morocco and Algeria at little cost to the Allies. The headquarters Eisenhower had formed and the subordinates he had shaped had performed their duties effectively. The first Anglo-American amphibious venture in the European theatre had gone well and had drawn the French in North Africa into the Allied camp.

For Eisenhower, the experience was rewarding. It gave him increased confidence in his abilities. It taught him the political complexities of warfare in the top echelons. It made him realize the loneliness and the awesome responsibilities of high command.

If he could take some measure of comfort in these positive gains, he was also dissatisfied because of his inability to give attention to the developing battle in Tunisia.

The French fleet at Toulon is scuttled to prevent the ships falling into German hands

Tunisia

German officers watch battle in Tunisia,
Rommel among them

While the Germans and Italians poured troops by plane and by ship from Sicily and Italy into Tunisia through the airfields and ports of Tunis and Bizerte, Anderson's Allied forces were moving eastward out of Algeria. Inevitably, the opposing sides met late in November. Although some of Anderson's units would come as close as fifteen miles to Tunis, they were stopped. The opponents then dug in, and the front became stabilized.

On Christmas Eve, Eisenhower admitted that he had lost what he would later term the 'pell-mell race for Tunisia'. Long distances, congested railroads, insufficient trucks, a lack of airfields, an absence of depots, a shortage of reserve units,

plus oncoming winter weather with rain and mud, had brought the eastward thrust to a halt. Eisenhower would have to wait two months at least, until the end of February, to continue the battle.

Only nine trains a day had been able to move from Algiers to the fighting front, and two of these had had to haul coal to run the railroad, while one had to carry food. This left six, and they were transporting troops as well as equipment and supplies. As a result, ammunition and rations, Eisenhower reported, were 'at the vanishing point'.

'I think the best way to describe our operations to date is that they have violated every recognized principle of war, are in conflict with all operational and logistic methods laid down in textbooks, and will be condemned, in their entirety, by all Leavenworth and War College classes for the next twenty-five years.'

In writing this, Eisenhower was being hard on himself. He had undertaken a calculated gamble, an attempt to get to Tunis and prevent Axis forces from entering Tunisia; and he had lost. As a consequence, he was 'like a caged tiger, snarling, and clawing to get things done.'

Still being criticized for the Darlan deal, Eisenhower was discouraged by the incessant rainfall in December. He was also disturbed by the difficulties that had arisen over the question of command in the field.

The French refused to serve under Anderson, a British officer. They would have accepted Eisenhower, but he was too far away in Algiers and too busy with political and administrative matters to exercise effective control over the battlefield. Thus, the enormous advantage of a unified command, which Eisenhower exemplified at AFHQ, vanished at the front.

British, American, and French combat and supply units became intermingled. The French were fighting among themselves, Americans and British were quarreling with each

Above : Junkers transports ferry matériel to Tunisia
Below : French reinforcements arrive by train

Lieutenant-General Anderson; the French objected to serving under a British commander

other. All were adversely affected by the unexpected Axis opposition, the awful conditions in the field that came mainly from the weather, and the shortages of men, equipment, and supplies.

'The abandonment for the time being of our plan for a full-out effort, [toward Tunis]' Eisenhower informed the Combined Chiefs on 24th December, 'has been the severest disappointment I have suffered to date.'

That night, a young Frenchman assassinated Darlan. The principal deterrent to completely cordial relations among French, Americans, and British was now removed. Giraud replaced Darlan to the joy of Roosevelt and Churchill, who were delighted that the apparent tie to Vichy had vanished. Although De Gaulle had only contempt for Giraud, he could work with him, and French unity was now possible.

The arrival in January 1943 of Harold Macmillan to work with Murphy – both were Eisenhower's political advisers – also took political burdens off Eisenhower's mind. As Allied commander, he was the only man through whom a whole variety of British and American agencies could implement their policies in North Africa, and through him flowed a continual flood of directives and advice and requests for information from the Combined Chiefs, the American Joint Chiefs, the State Department, the War Department, the Foreign Office, the White House, and Downing Street. 'We have a military occupation in North Africa,' Roosevelt said, 'and as such our Commanding General [Eisenhower] has complete charge of all matters civil as well as military.'

He could and did delegate authority to various of his assistants and adivsers, but he was unable to delegate the ultimate responsibility for whatever they did. Although the vast problems of administration and policy continued to weigh heavily on him, he was able at the turn of the year to give greater attention to the more military aspects of his tasks, specifically, the military operations in Tunisia.

He began to concentrate on building up the fighting forces, sorting them out into separate national sectors, creating adequate reserves, constructing proper lines of communications, and straightening out the command situation.

The front consisted of British forces in the northern part of Tunisia, French troops in the centre – operating for the most part in mountainous terrain where their obsolete equipment was less a handicap – and American units in the south. Several tours of inspection impressed Eisenhower with the material weakness of the French and with the training deficiencies of the Americans.

The Americans were overconfident after having come ashore in North Africa so easily, and they believed that the Germans would melt away upon their approach. Physically soft,

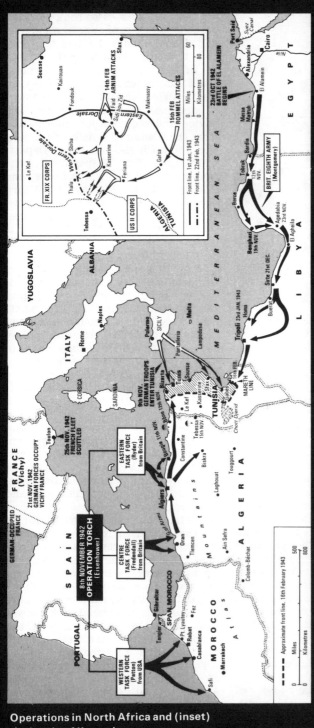

**Operations in North Africa and (inset)
the battle of Kasserine**

Rommel (right) discusses the military position

unable to operate efficiently off the few roads, incapable of displaying the toughness required in combat, inexperienced and understrength, the Americans were in for a rude shock.

Trying to cushion what he was sure would be a harsh awakening, Eisenhower encouraged his subordinate commanders to prepare their troops for the realities of the battle that would develop in the spring. 'I cannot urge too strongly,' he reiterated, 'that emphasis be placed on individual and small unit training.'

Eisenhower was concerned too because the front was so thin. He was unhappy about Fredendall's propensity for remaining in his command post rather than visiting the front – Fredendall's headquarters was in an underground command post dug into rock and located far to the rear. And Eisenhower was not pleased with the unsatisfactory degree of cooperation Anderson was able to get from the Americans and the French.

All these deficiencies in the com-

mand structure on the battlefield, all the bickering among the Allies, and all the shortages in manpower and supplies would soon have disastrous results.

Pulling back skillfully ahead of Montgomery's pursuing elements, Rommel moved across Libya. Early in 1943, he reached the border between Libya and Tunisia. There, in defensive positions the French had built, the Mareth Line, Rommel finally brought his withdrawal to a close.

Montgomery was still after him, but the British would require some time before they could bring substantial troop units forward and attempt to pry Rommel loose from the fortified Mareth Line.

While he waited for Montgomery to move up against the Mareth positions, Rommel discovered the conditions for an attack westward into Tunisia and against Eisenhower's

Kasserine Pass, where Allied armor was severely mauled

forces. This would later be known as the Battle of Kasserine Pass. There, Rommel would teach the Allies, and particularly the Americans, a shocking lesson.

Members of the Allied high command – the President, the Prime Minister, and the Combined Chiefs of Staff – met in Casablanca in January, 1943, for a full-scale review of global strategy. Although the discussions ranged around the world, much of the talk revolved about the question of what to do after the campaign in North Africa, assuming, of course, that Eisenhower eventually cleared the north shore of the African continent.

The British were interested in maintaining the momentum generated by TORCH, and they wished to continue operations somewhere in the Mediterranean region. The Americans were badly divided in their strategic wishes – Roosevelt liked Sicily and

Italy as targets for invasion after North Africa, while Marshall kept calling for a cross-Channel attack.

The upshot was an agreement, somewhat half-hearted on the part of the Americans, to carry the war to Sicily in 1943. This would make use of the troops already assembled in North Africa at the end of the Tunisian campaign, troops that would otherwise remain idle or have to be transported to another theater. But this meant that a cross-Channel attack would be impossible before 1944.

Eisenhower was asked to appear before the top military leaders in Casablanca, and he reported on his operations in Tunisia. He was followed by Alexander, who gave the political and military chiefs a briefing on the operations against Rommel in Libya.

At Eisenhower's suggestion, the Combined Chiefs separated ETOUSA from North Africa. Favorably impressed with the way Eisenhower was running his show and particularly pleased with the surprising effectiveness of AFHQ, the Combined Chiefs

decided to bring together under a single command the forces under Alexander and those under Eisenhower. When the British Eighth Army reached the Tunisian border and was in firm contact with Rommel at the Mareth Line, an event expected sometime in February, the two theaters would be joined. Alexander would become subordinate to Eisenhower as the Allied ground forces commander. Eisenhower would now be, unquestionably, the Supreme Allied Commander.

As Brooke explained later, Eisenhower would be boosted 'into the stratosphere and rarefied atmosphere of a Supreme Commander, where he would be free to devote his time to the political and inter-allied problems'. In the meantime, a triumvirate of British commanders operating immediately below Eisenhower – Alexander on the ground, Tedder in the air, and Cunningham at sea – would actually deal with the military situations.

On this basis, Eisenhower might

The Casablanca Conference of January 1943 ; left to right : Giraud, President Roosevelt, de Gaulle, Churchill. Global strategy, and particularly events in North Africa, are discussed

have simply accepted the rôle of a real chairman of the board, while letting his subordinates make the decisions that counted. But he was convinced that command by committee, which was the British system, would be impossible, particularly where Americans were concerned. Despite the form of the British concept to be employed, Eisenhower would insist on the American principle of unified command. All decisions, he would make certain, would ultimately be made by his authority, and he would remain ultimately responsible for them. Through the power of his personal force of character, he would see that Alexander, Tedder, and Cunningham recognized him as the Supreme Allied Commander in fact and that they

Juergen von Arnim, in command of the mixed force of German and Italian troops around Bizerte and Tunis

Commander of 1st Armored Division, Orlando Ward. Eisenhower was concerned by reports of friction between Ward and his superior Fredendall

obeyed his wishes. He would be, without any qualifications, the boss.

Early in 1943 the opponents in Tunisia were lined up along the Eastern Dorsale, a range of mountains roughly paralleling the eastern shore of the country. In the north, around Bizerte and Tunis, was an Italo-German army under Juergen von Arnim. In the south, in the Mareth Line, was Rommel's army.

On the other side of the Dorsale were the Allies. They controlled the few passes through the mountains, but they lacked the strength to try to move eastward to the sea, to Sousse or Sfax on the coast, thereby severing contact between Arnim and Rommel.

This rather quiet state of affairs was broken on 1st February, when German troops suddenly struck a small French force holding the Faid pass. The Germans dispersed the French and seized the passage through the Eastern Dorsale. Having done so, they subsided.

Although the situation again lapsed into an uneasy equilibrium, the German threat at Faid was unmistakable. Given the relatively few Allied troops on the front and the slowness of Montgomery's approach toward the Mareth positions, the Germans

were bound to strike again. Where they would do so, if indeed they did, became a matter of immediate and grave concern.

Eisenhower's G-2 alerted him to the possibility that the Germans were planning to attack. According to information gathered from a variety of intelligence sources, the Germans, the G-2 said, would thrust into the Allied lines in the north.

Upon news of this development, Eisenhower visited the combat troops on 12th February. He was interested in inspecting the defensive arrangements. He was curious also to see at first hand whether certain reports that had reached him were true. These detailed the animosity that existed between two American commanders, Fredendall who headed the II Corps, and one of his immediate subordinates, Orlando Ward, who commanded the 1st Armored Division.

During the afternoon of 13th February, Eisenhower visited Fredendall in his elaborate and well dug-in command post near Tebessa. Anderson came to report to Eisenhower there, and he said that he expected the Germans to attack, not in Fredendall's sector, but in the north. This

feeling on Anderson's part coincided with the belief of Eisenhower's G-2, and immediately after the conference, Anderson hurried back to his headquarters.

Fredendall scoffed at Anderson's information. He anticipated an attack in his area, in the southern portion of the front. Although he had made arrangements to meet a German thrust, he had been unable to persuade Anderson to send him American troops (stationed in the north, where Anderson believed he would need them).

Somewhat disquieted by the lack of cooperation between Anderson and Fredendall, Eisenhower went forward that afternoon to the American front-line positions held by Ward and his men. To Eisenhower these troops appeared green and inexperienced; they had yet to meet German combat units.

That night, after he had been briefed on the measures that had been taken to meet a German offensive, Eisenhower went for a short walk into

Fredendall discusses strategy with French officers

the desert. It was close to midnight. The moon had appeared, and the scene near Sidi bou Zid was beautiful. Intuitively, Eisenhower had a feeling that all was not so quiet as appearances suggested. And indeed, he had no way of knowing that the Germans around the Faid pass were preparing to deliver a bloody valentine at dawn.

Eisenhower returned to Tebessa, just across the border in Algeria, during the dark and early morning hours of 14th February. He was accompanied by Lucian Truscott, who acted as Eisenhower's representative at Constantine, which was somewhat closer to the front than Algiers. Truscott's duties were to keep Eisenhower informed of what was happening on the front and to keep Anderson and the other combat leaders informed of Eisenhower's wishes.

When they reached Tebessa and Fredendall's command post, they

US armor prepares for the conflict

learned that the Germans had launched an attack at Sidi bou Zid. It seemed like a small effort.

Continuing his trip back to Constantine, Eisenhower, together with Truscott, left the main road to visit Roman ruins at Timgad. In mid-afternoon, the two officers reached their destination. They found word that the skirmish at Sidi bou Zid had developed into a real battle. That evening news came that the American troops had suffered a disastrous defeat. Half of the 1st Armored Division had been lost.

Eisenhower at once gave Anderson permission to pull back from the Eastern Dorsale. But he told Anderson to be sure to stand fast at the Western Dorsale in order to protect Tebessa, an Allied supply centre, and more importantly Le Kef, where the main Allied depots were located. If Le Kef were lost, Bone and Algiers would become possible German objectives,

and the entire Allied position in French North-West Africa would be threatened.

Instead of returning to Algiers, Eisenhower remained at Constantine. While the Allied soldiers, British, French, and American, tried to stem the German offensive, which developed into a fierce attack staged by Rommel, Eisenhower shored up the front by getting units, equipment, weapons, and supplies forward from Algeria. Pressuring his subordinates for action cutting red tape, he personally looked after arrangements for getting more strength to the battlefield.

A week later the Germans had moved fifty miles forward to the Western Dorsale and were trying to get through the Kasserine Pass. If they broke through, they would have access both to Tebessa and to Le Kef.

At that point, Eisenhower lost confidence in Fredendall, who seemed uncertain how to direct the battle. Eisenhower turned to Clark, who had recently activated and taken com-

Brigadier-General Ernest Harmon. Eisenhower brought him to direct the battle having lost his trust in Fredendall's ability

mand of the US Fifth Army in Algeria. Clark was protecting the western border of Algeria against possible invasion by Franco's units from Spanish Morocco; he was also directing a large training program.

Would Clark take command of the II Corps in Tunisia? Eisenhower asked.

Clark felt that it would be unwise for him to step down from command of an army to take command of the lesser corps.

Eisenhower then called Ernest N Harmon, the commander of the 2nd Armored Division, which was in French Morocco. Harmon came from Casablanca, and went to Tunisia to help Fredendall.

It was a peculiar assignment that Eisenhower gave Harmon. Instead of placing Harmon in command of troops, he put him in command of the battle. The reason for his unorthodox action was Eisenhower's unwillingness to relieve Fredendall in the midst of the fight.

At the same time, Eisenhower asked that his G-2, a British officer, be relieved. The G-2, Eisenhower believed, had relied far too much on one particular kind of intelligence information and, as a consequence, had failed to note the concentration of German troops at Faid at the outset of the enemy offensive.

At Kasserine Pass, Rommel was finally blocked. Concerned with Montgomery's approach to the Mareth Line, and believing that he could no longer defeat the strengthened Allies, Rommel decided to withdraw. Pulling his forces back from the Western Dorsale, he hurried back to the Mareth positions. The start of that withdrawal began, and it started imperceptibly, on the day that Harmon arrived at the front.

Sensing that Rommel was about to retire, Eisenhower urged his subordinate commanders to counterattack immediately. Those at the front were too wary to do so, and Harmon, who was one of the most aggressive American leaders, lacked thorough knowledge of the conditions to carry the battle into an immediate offensive. Still suffering from the rude shock administered by the Desert Fox, Anderson and Fredendall waited for surer indication of Rommel's intention. As a result, they let Rommel escape.

Had they reacted as positively as Eisenhower wished, had they been able to instill confidence in their battered troops, they might have eliminated Rommel's army and thus brought the Tunisian campaign to a quicker end.

At the close of the battle of Kasserine Pass, Harmon, who had restored a sense of confidence among his American colleagues, returned to Constantine and talked with Eisenhower. He recommended that Fredendall be relieved because Fredendall lacked the steadiness and aggressiveness needed by combat commanders.

Eisenhower asked Harmon to take command of II Corps, but Harmon felt it would be unethical for him to do so after he had recommended Fredendall's relief. He suggested Patton.

Above : Men of the 8th Field Squadron, Royal Engineers, probe for mines on the Thala-Kasserine road
Below : A Mareth Line strongpoint abandoned during the Allied advance

Above : Rommel gives up the assault on Kasserine Pass ; German equipment litters the battlefield. *Below :* Patton is called from Morocco to take command of II Corps

Calling Patton from Morocco and giving him command of the corps, Eisenhower instructed him: 'You must not retain for one instant any man in a responsible position where you have become doubtful of his ability to do the job . . . This matter frequently calls for more courage than any other thing you will have to do, but I expect you to be perfectly cold-blooded about it.'

Eisenhower ordered Patton to rehabilitate the corps, to restore pride among the American soldiers who had taken a terrible lacing, and to improve American combat efficiency. He told Patton that he would not tolerate further bickering between British and Americans. 'The great purpose of complete Allied teamwork must be achieved in this theater.'

The image of the American fighting man had suffered at Kasserine, and this was a matter of concern to Eisenhower, especially because Alexander had become the Allied ground

Eisenhower at his meeting with General Alexander, Commander British First Army, and Patton

American equipment, including Sherman tanks, helps the British compete on equal terms

commander in the midst of that battle. During his first contact with American combat troops, Alexander saw them at their worst, at a time when many were panic-stricken and fleeing. Since Alexander would in large part determine the assignments of the ground force units under him, he would certainly be right to use the Americans for subsidiary operations unless they improved.

When Alexander drew his plan for the final elimination of the Bizerte-Tunis bridgehead, he projected an offensive that would squeeze the Americans out of the line and let the British drive for the final victory.

This, Eisenhower told him, would have 'unfortunate results as to national prestige,' and he opposed Alexander's plan. Beginning to have doubts about Alexander's fairness toward Americans and satisfied that Patton had rehabilitated American combat effectiveness, Eisenhower told Alexander bluntly that Americans had

47

to have their own sector in the final phase of the Tunisian campaign.

In protest, Alexander pointed out that the Americans had failed at Kasserine Pass.

Eisenhower then explained the facts to Alexander. The Americans had given British units in North Africa some of their best equipment, including the newly-developed Sherman tank, which the Americans might have used themselves at Kasserine Pass instead of continuing to fight with inferior weapons. Furthermore, if the American people learned that Alexander was operating in a manner prejudicial to the American troops, they would insist on shifting their main effort at once to the Pacific. What Alexander had to do was to permit the Americans to regain their confidence, to make it possible for them to develop their feeling that they could fight the Germans and beat them.

Alexander admitted that Eisenhower was right. In the final battle that cleared North Africa of Axis troops, American and British units fought shoulder to shoulder, both sharing in a victory that ended with the loss of more Axis troops than the Germans had lost at Stalingrad.

By May 1943 the Axis forces had been entirely cleared from North Africa.

The main ingredient in the Allied victory was Eisenhower's insistence on welding together an Allied team that would reveal in subsequent operations how closely knit the alliance was. There had been a close brush at Kasserine Pass. But this too had provided valuable experience. As Eisenhower informed Marshall: 'All our people from the very highest to the very lowest have learned [from Kasserine] that this is not a child's game and [they] are ready and eager to get down to the fundamental business of profiting by the lessons they have learned and seeking from every possible source methods and means of perfecting their own battle-

field efficiency . . . [The troops] are now mad and ready to fight.'

Eisenhower too had been mad at the spectacle of American troops running from the enemy. What he learned from Kasserine was that training must never stop in a theater of operations. He also came to realize the importance of unity of command at every level. And he determined that he would never permit divisions to be broken up on the battlefield; divisions were organic units organized to do specific jobs, and they had to be fought as complete and intact organizations.

Finally, as he told his friend

Leonard Gerow, who was training an infantry division in Scotland: 'Officers that fail . . . must be ruthlessly weeded out. Considerations of friendship, family, kindliness and nice personality have nothing whatsoever to do with the problem . . . you must be tough [and get rid of the] lazy, the slothful, the indifferent or the complacent.'

He was really talking to himself. If he seemed to remain the pleasant, affable commander, he was in reality underneath it all tough and driving. Victory was too precarious a prize to suffer anything but efficient leadership

Italian and German prisoners. The Axis powers lost more troops in North Africa than at Stalingrad

and effective performance.

Although Eisenhower seemed to have remained remote from the battlefield in Tunisia, his presence had been directly felt by all who had worked under him. He had forged a single-minded, yet flexible approach to the problems of coalition warfare. Although he had suffered a near-disaster in Tunisia, he had recovered with no loss of nerve or will. His influence would continue to grow.

49

Sicily

Coming ashore on Italian soil

The problem of how to get ashore in Sicily, an invasion approved by the Combined Chiefs of Staff at the Casablanca Conference, provoked almost endless discussion. Messina, the city in the north-eastern corner of the island and only a few miles from the Italian mainland, was the obvious strategic objective, for if Messina were taken, the German and Italian troops on the island would be trapped, unable to escape to the Italian toe.

Yet Messina was well fortified, protected by what seemed to Allied pilots to be a wall of anti-aircraft fire and also by a swarm of interceptor aircraft based on nearby airfields. Sailing into the strait of Messina would be dangerous for Allied warships because of numerous coastal

guns. Finally, there seemed to be no beaches in the vicinity suitable for amphibious landings.

The British were particularly cautious about invading Sicily, and British planners stressed the necessity of securing airfields and ports before driving to Messina. As a consequence, the first plan issued by Alexander, who would be responsible for the ground forces to be employed there, set up three separate landings – one in the south-eastern part of the island, a second near the south-western corner, and the third somewhere in the north-west. It was a complicated design that would give logisticians headaches, particularly since it envisioned three successive assaults instead of three simultaneous landings. Dispersing the Allied strength on three fronts, it would make each vulnerable to defeat in detail.

Montgomery, who would lead his Eighth Army into Sicily, protested that the forces available to the Allies were not strong enough to take all the objectives laid out in the three-landing plan. He wanted to concentrate the Allied strength, and he requested that an American division be assigned to work under his command. This meant eliminating the south-western landing near Gela.

Opposing Montgomery were Cunningham and Tedder, who felt that many landings would stretch the Axis defenders. The Italians were poorly equipped and low in morale, but they might fight well in defence of Italian soil. If the Germans entered Sicily in large numbers, they would be difficult to defeat.

Ultimately, there were eight separate plans worked out for the Sicilian invasion. Eisenhower had no specific responsibility for the final plan accepted, but he visited the subordinate headquarters – Alexander's, Cunningham's, and Tedder's – and by conversation and suggestion helped develop the final concept. Eisenhower's tendency was to follow Montgomery's advice and urge a con-

Montgomery, British Eighth Army
Commander. He insisted that the Allied
effort in Sicily would be too dispersed
with the forces available

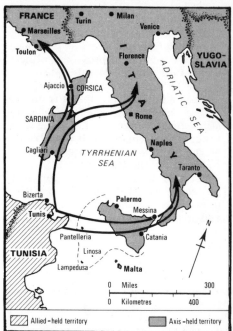

Plans for the invasion of Italy

centrated assault rather than a dispersed invasion. This would reduce the risks inherent in all amphibious assaults and permit the British and American forces to give each other mutual support.

While planning for Sicily was in progress, the Combined Chiefs of Staff, together with Churchill and Roosevelt, met in Washington in May. They discussed what ought to be done beyond Sicily. The British were anxious to continue the momentum in the Mediterranean, and they looked to a full-scale descent on the Italian mainland. The Americans were still thinking of a cross-Channel attack, although they recognized that they had to reinforce success in the Mediterranean. Hoping to gain both ends, they favoured developing Mediterranean operations beyond Sicily in the direction of southern France. This meant going from Sicily to Sardinia and Corsica.

After much debate, the Combined Chiefs decided to execute a cross-Channel attack in the spring of 1944.

In 1943, they would try to eliminate Italy from the war.

They still left up in the air the question of where to go once Sicily was conquered. How was Eisenhower to eliminate Italy?

In the absence of firm agreement among the partners and consequently in the absence of firm guidance to Eisenhower, Marshall suggested that Eisenhower set up two separate planning headquarters, each to plan a different operation – one for landings in Sardinia and Corsica, the other for an invasion of southern Italy. Depending on how the campaign in Sicily went, depending on what happened to Italian morale – would it deteriorate to the point of collapse or would the Italians fight hard? – the Combined Chiefs would make the decision on where to go after Sicily.

That was, of course, all in the future. At the moment, early in the

Alexander and Eisenhower discuss the landings

Pantelleria capitulates after heavy bombardment

summer of 1943, the Sicilian invasion was all-important. What bothered the Allied planners was the impossibility of providing sufficient air cover to the invading troops. Because Sicily was beyond the acceptable range for fighter aircraft based in North Africa, the Axis air forces would have a decided advantage.

To overcome this disability, Eisenhower suggested that the Allies take the island of Pantelleria as a preliminary to Sicily. Pantelleria and its satellite isles of Lampedusa and Linoso were Italian possessions, and Mussolini had turned them into airfields and had fortified them. If the Allies had Pantelleria and could base their own planes there, they could furnish a better amount of air cover to the troops coming ashore in Sicily.

Alexander and most of the other of Eisenhower's subordinates argued against an operation to take Pantelleria. The island was highly fortified

and was regarded as virtually invulnerable to invasion. There was only one small harbour where a landing could be made, and it was well protected by coastal guns. The rest of the shoreline was rocky, providing no beaches for troops emerging from landing ships and craft. Finally, the general shortage of Allied troops in the Mediterranean theatre made it necessary to draw upon the forces earmarked for Sicily if Pantelleria was to be invaded. Success seemed hardly likely.

Eisenhower proposed that Pantelleria be bombed into submission. He suggested that the Allies institute a kind of laboratory experiment to see exactly how effective air bombing was. If the proponents of air power were accurate in their forecasts of what bombers could do, and if the weight of naval power were thrown in to help plaster Pantelleria, the island's defences might be smashed and the airfields taken without actual ground fighting. A British division could simply sail into the harbour and occupy the territory.

Over the protests of his subordinates, this is what Eisenhower ordered.

For three weeks, Allied planes blasted Pantelleria. There was no sign of surrender from the island's defenders. Warships shelled the island in a mighty display of naval gun power. Still there appeared no dent in the island's defences, no indication of a willingness to capitulate.

Early in June, as the British airborne division made ready to sail from North Africa to Pantelleria, the division commander pointed out to Alexander that he expected the operation to fail; he feared awful casualties, for Pantelleria was a Gibraltar in miniature.

Alexander relayed this feeling to Eisenhower. Given the bristling guns on Pantelleria and the immense thickness of the concrete protecting troop and headquarters installations, a full-scale invasion was necessary to take it. Anything less than an all-out effort would never work.

Eisenhower disagreed. He insisted that the operation be carried out as he had projected it.

On 11th June, when the British troops set sail, Eisenhower, despite his unruffled exterior, was unusually concerned. He might, after all, be wrong about Pantelleria. According to his aide, who made the notation in his diary at the time, Eisenhower 'has been going through the same type of jitters and worries which marked the days immediately preceding our landings in North Africa.'

After a final naval pounding and air strike, the British ground troops descended from their transports and into landing ships and craft. The island was obscured by smoke and dust as they made their way toward the harbor of Pantelleria. As they neared the shore, before a single soldier had set foot on soil, the Italians surrendered.

With Pantelleria, Lampedusa, and Linoso in Allied possession, the air-

Eighth Army troops about to leave North Africa for Sicily

Dawn landings on Sicily. Working parties prepare roads from the shore for trucks and other traffic

fields were quickly rehabilitated, Allied fighters were quickly flown in, and the projected invasion of Sicily had a much better chance of success because of the consequent air cover.

Eisenhower's plan, on which he had insisted despite widespread doubts, had worked.

The invasion of Sicily, codenamed HUSKY, was the largest amphibious assault in history in terms of the number of ground troops initially employed and in terms of frontage. Seven divisions, plus parts of two airborne divisions, would come ashore along a front of one hundred miles in length.

The big questions before the invasion were the state of the weather and the state of Italian morale.

To be as close as possible to the scene of the action, Eisenhower on 7th July went to Malta, where Cunningham's command post was located. At the last minute, the weather turned bad. High winds and large waves threw planes and ships off course. Some of Eisenhower's subordinates urged postponing the operation, but a delay would require a two- or three-week deferment until the invasion fleets could be reformed and restaged. Eisenhower conferred with his meteorologists. When he learned that the weather was expected to improve immediately before the scheduled time of the landings, he gave the go-ahead sign. 'The operation will proceed as scheduled,' Eisenhower wired Marshall.

Despite the better weather promised by the meteorologists, the winds and high seas continued to make the invasion a matter of concern up to the last moment. All the units in the landings experienced difficulties. Yet they managed to get ashore with relatively light losses. The reason was the erratic and generally in-

effective resistance on the part of the Italian defenders. Although the Allies expected the Italian troops to have high morale, the Italian opposition inflicted relatively few casualties on the Allied forces.

The subsequent fighting was to be harder, for the Germans reinforced the Italians, and they would use the terrain to extreme advantage, fighting skillfully. They would hold the Allies up for more than a month.

For the most part, the conquest of the island of Sicily was conducted by Eisenhower's subordinate commanders. Alexander directed the ground forces, Cunningham the fleets, and Tedder the air cover. To some extent there was a lack of coordination among the three services, but this was due to a large extent to the separation of headquarters – Cunningham was on Malta, Tedder was in Tunisia, and Alexander moved to Sicily.

More important than this, there was friction between the two army

Italian soldiers surrender in Sicily. The German forces proved more determined

commanders on the island. Patton commanded the US Seventh Army, Montgomery the British Eighth. Still conditioned by his view of the American fighting man at Kasserine Pass, Alexander laid out the campaign so that Montgomery and the British would make the major effort; he relegated Patton and the Americans to a protective mission, securing Montgomery's flank.

The landings had been clustered around the south-eastern point of the island, and the British were to drive up the eastern coast from Syracuse through Catania to Messina, while the Americans on the left protected the British movement.

It was for this reason that an outraged Patton pushed hard to Palermo, then raced for Messina. He managed to beat Montgomery, who had been held up at Catania, into the port city, the capture of which marked the end

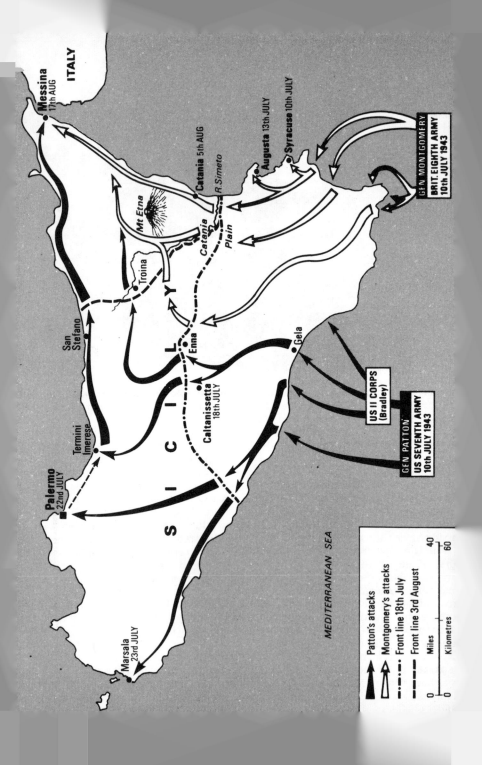

of the campaign.

In the process, the American combat troops regained their confidence both in their efficiency and in their ability to meet and overcome the German forces.

Although Eisenhower took little active part in the campaign, leaving the operational decisions to his subordinates, he was the driving force behind the growing maturity of the American combat forces. He shook down the Allied command. He proved also at Sicily that new amphibious techniques, particularly the concept of beach unloading, were feasible, and they would become standard.

Handling for the most part diplomatic, strategic, and administrative duties, Eisenhower nevertheless kept close watch on the battlefield. He preferred to give his subordinates a free hand. But, as he wrote that summer, 'when the time comes that he himself [the Supreme Commander] feels he must make a decision, he must make it in clean-cut fashion and on his own responsibility and take full blame for anything that goes wrong whether or not it results from his

Patton in Sicily. Here occurred the notorious 'slapping incident' which threatened to hold up Patton's promotion

mistake or from an error on the part of a subordinate . . . He is in a very definite sense the Chairman of a Board, a Chairman that has very definite responsibilities . . . He must execute those duties firmly, wisely and without any question as to his own authority and his own responsibility.'

This characterized his own view of his duties as Supreme Allied Commander.

Probably the most celebrated event in the Sicilian campaign was the slapping incident that involved Patton, one of Eisenhower's longest friends and certainly one of America's greatest combat leaders. On two occasions, while visiting hospitals on the island, Patton was intensely moved by the sufferings of the wounded. Twice this highly emotional and perhaps overwrought man cursed and slapped soldiers who were afflicted with nervous depression or shell shock.

The doctors were astonished and angered by Patton's behavior, and two days afterwards, they sent a report to Omar N Bradley, II Corps commander. Since Bradley was directly under Patton, the only action he could have taken would have been to send it to his superior, Patton. Since the report concerned Patton's behavior, Bradley locked it in his safe.

Learning that no corrective action could be expected by going through the command channels, the doctors sent a report of Patton's acts through medical channels. By this route, the report reached Eisenhower's theater Surgeon General, a member of Eisenhower's staff. This medical officer delivered it to the Supreme Commander.

It was 17th August, and Patton had just entered Messina. Elated that the campaign had ended, Eisenhower's immediate reaction to the report of the Patton incident was a remark he made to the Surgeon General: 'I guess I'll have to give General Patton a jacking up.'

He then asked his Surgeon General to go to Sicily and to make a complete investigation, but to keep it quiet because Patton was, Eisenhower said, 'indispensable to the war effort – one of the guarantors of our victory.'

When Eisenhower learned beyond question that the slapping incidents had actually occurred, he wrote a personal letter to Patton. 'I clearly understand,' he said, 'that firm and drastic measures are at times necessary in order to secure desired objectives, but this does not excuse brutality, abuse of the sick, nor exhibition of uncontrollable temper in front of subordinates.' He was proud of Patton's success in the field, but he had to 'seriously question your good judgement and your self-discipline.' He ordered Patton to apologize to the soldiers and to the nurses and the doctors. He would not, he told Patton, tolerate further conduct of this sort.

Patton did as he was required. He apologized to all who had heard and seen him in the hospitals. He then wrote Eisenhower a pathetic letter of regret.

When reporters heard the story, they took the matter up with Eisenhower and demanded that he relieve Patton. Eisenhower begged them to keep the story quiet so that Patton could be 'saved for the great battles facing us in Europe'.

The war correspondents entered into a gentleman's agreement to sit on the incidents. Later, when a journalist came into the theater and picked up the story, he felt he had no obligation to remain silent. He broadcast the news in November, and shook the American public. Against a flood of letters demanding Patton's relief, Eisenhower insisted that Patton was invaluable to the American war effort. His driving aggressiveness was unique, and to lose him for the remainder of the war would have jeopardized the prospects for quick and thorough victory.

Eisenhower saved Patton's career and preserved his talents for the critical final battles in Europe. How right Eisenhower was to keep him would become stunningly apparent in the summer of 1944, when Patton fashioned triumphs of an unprecedented nature.

What the slapping incident produced was Eisenhower's selection of Bradley over Patton to go to England in September as commander of the US First Army. Bradley, not Patton, would head up the American forces getting ready to execute the cross-Channel attack in the spring of 1944.

Patton remained in Sicily with no active rôle except to enhance a variety of Allied deception plans. During the remainder of 1943, Patton traveled extensively throughout the Mediterranean area to make the Germans believe that he was about to lead an invasion force somewhere or other.

By then, the Allies had invaded southern Italy.

Washington Post

Second Mighty Raid Strikes Paralyzed, Burning Berlin; Makin Falls, Reports Nimitz

Tarawa Seizure Sure; Situation On Abemama 'Well in Hand'

Navy Wants Money

NAVY REQUESTS five billion dollars additional for landing craft and auxiliary vessels. Page 5.

Power in Pacific

Pearl Harbor, T. H., Nov. 23 (AP).—Success of the first American offensive of the war in the central Pacific is assured. Admiral Chester W. Nimitz announced triumphantly today.

Already the Twenty-seventh Division has captured Makin Atoll. The capture of Tarawa, where the Marines have consolidated their positions, is certain. Amphibious forces cracked the beach defenses of both places last Saturday.

The situation on Abemama Atoll, 80 miles south of Tarawa, was reported well in hand. The Marines' landing there was announced only yesterday.

(Eugene Burns, Associated Press correspondent, declared that the forces attacking the atoll included the greatest aircraft force ever assembled in the Pacific—Editor's note.)

An excellent bomber field within striking distance of strong Japanese bases in the Marshall Islands to the north will become available with the capture of Tarawa. Fighting on Tarawa was believed to be confined to Betio Island, which has air base facilities. The enemy was strongly entrenched on Betio, at the southwestern tail of Tarawa Atoll. The island is a sand waste less than 2 miles long and about a 1000 yards wide.

Progress Reported

The Marines were making good progress on Betio, where it was indicated they had landed on the western end of the islet and had pushed the Nipponese back to the eastern portion.

Makin, to the north of Tarawa, is entirely in American hands, a fleet spokesman said. Forces there were engaged in mopping up and in cleaning out snipers.

The fleet spokesman indicated there were four or five thousand Japanese on Tarawa, where the stiffest resistance was encountered from the outset.

"Approximately twice as many as were on Attu (where there were more than 2000) and five times as many as on Makin," was the way he put it.

He did not say whether all these troops were concentrated on Betio or whether other islands of the atoll were garrisoned. It was obvious, however, that the bulk of the Japanese strength in the Tarawa atoll was on Betio.

no com-
See Sec-
umn 5

Patton Hit Shell-Shocked Man, Eisenhower Forced an Apology

Seventh Army Head's Superior Called Conduct 'Despicable'

By Edward Kennedy
Allied Headquarters, Algiers, Nov. 23 (AP).—Lieut. Gen. George S. Patton, Jr., who led the American Seventh Army through a brilliant conquest of Sicily, at the close of that offensive apologized in person to his Army for having struck a shell-shocked soldier in a hospital tent in a fit of rage while the campaign was in a critical stage.

The incident led to an investigation to determine whether animosity of his men toward Patton was so great as to impair his usefulness as a commander. This investigation apparently convinced Gen. Dwight D. Eisenhower and the War Department that this was not the case, as Patton retained his command and was nominated by the President to be promoted in his permanent Army rank to major general.

Sunday night, in comment on a broadcast by Columnist Drew Pearson, an official headquarters statement was issued saying:

"General Patton is commanding the Seventh Army, has commanded it since it was activated and is continuing to command it. General Patton has never been reprimanded at any time by General Eisenhower or by anyone else in this theater."

Three-Month-Old Incident

Although today's statement bore out that Patton had not, indeed, been officially reprimanded, correspondents were permitted to tell what did happen.

The incident was disclosed officially by Allied headquarters today 3½ months after it occurred. Behind the headquarters announcement is one of the strangest war stories ever told.

It is a tale of a general, whose merit is recognized by everyone, slapping and swearing at a distraught soldier whom he believed to be a malingerer and denouncing the soldier as a coward before other soldiers who lay wounded in their cots.

As it turned out, the soldier in question was not a coward, but a 24-year-old Southern boy with an excellent record who had gone through the grimmest fighting of the Tunisian and Sicilian campaigns and who had left the front only when ordered out by the doctor. The soldier, on being called a coward by his commanding general, felt that his whole world had disintegrated.

General Eisenhower, upon hearing of the incident, immediately wrote Patton a letter in which he denounced his conduct and ordered

See PATTON, Page 2, Column 1

Sicilian Incident Likely to Hold Up Officer's Promotion

Disclosure that Lieut. Gen. George S. Patton struck a shell-shocked soldier in a Sicilian hospital threatened yesterday to hold up indefinitely Senate confirmation or Patton's promotion from colonel to the permanent rank of major general.

Ranking members of both House and Senate Military Committees said they would oppose any formal congressional investigation of the incident, on the grounds that the Army has full jurisdiction, but the general's conduct was severely criticized on both sides of the Capitol.

A member of the Senate Military Committee, who asked not to be named, said "there isn't a chance" now that the committee will approve or the Senate will confirm Patton's October 1 nomination for a permanent increase in Army rank.

May Come Up Today

Both House and Senate committees had scheduled meetings this morning on other business, but members said the Sicilian incident inevitably will come up.

The name of "Old Blood and Guts" heads the list of permanent Army promotion nominations sent to the Senate the first of last month. Action had been temporarily delayed because some of the Army officers on the list (not Patton) lacked the requisite 28 years' experience for permanent general's rank. Legislation has been hurried through the Senate to remove the service requirement, and was the first order of business before the House Military Affairs Committee today.

Representative Paul J. Kilday (Democrat) of Texas said questions on Patton's Army seniority (he was commissioned a second lieutenant

See ARMY, Page 6, Column 5

Battered From Its Center to Suburbs, City Gets No Respite

London (Wednesday), Nov. 24 (AP).—A mighty force of RAF bombers was reported today to have pounded Berlin for the second successive night last night as the German capital lay smashed and smoking from a 1000-bomber raid which hurled more than 2300 long tons of high explosives and incendiaries on the Nazi capital Monday night.

Germany's radio Zeesen announced last night's attack after British watchers saw the bombers cross the coast in a procession which took 45 minutes to pass.

The Reich capital, a city of 332 square miles, was still smoking from the greatest aerial blow ever struck in warfare when the German announcer took the air to say the new attack was expected "and special defense precautions were taken."

The weather favored the defense more than the previous night, the radio said and it declared that a "considerable number of attacking planes were shot down."

There were indications that last night's assault, the third on Berlin in the last six days, might be as

LIEUT. GEN. GEORGE S. PATTON, Jr.

Count Bernadotte Finds 'Total War' in Berlin Raid

Stockholm, Nov. 23 (AP).—Count Bernadotte, nephew of King Gustav V of Sweden, who was caught in last night's RAF raid on Berlin while traveling from a Geneva Red Cross meeting to Stockholm, said tonight "now I know what total war means."

heavy as the history-making 77-ton-per-minute bombing of the previous night.

The Allies did last night what the Germans once dreamed of doing to London, but on five times the scale the Germans ever attained.

The record raid on the Nazi capital, which Germans leaders once boasted never would feel the terror of Allied bombs, was made despite bad weather, and the huge black night bombers of the RAF flying through thick clouds not only smashed the industrial suburbs but hit government buildings in the great city with their record weight of explosives. The previous record weight of just 2300 long tons poured down on Hamburg last August 23.

Reports tonight from Stockholm said a heavy pall of smoke hung over the stricken Nazi capital all day, and tonight parts of the city still were in flames with fire-fighters and other air raid workers already weary from coping with a heavy attack four nights before, still toiling desperately

British Repulse Heavy Nazi Counterattack

8th Army Seizes Strategic Town, Algiers Radio Says

By Noland Norgaard
Allied Headquarters, Algiers, Nov. 23 (AP).—Charging before a backdrop of burning towns and villages being destroyed in a "scorched earth" withdrawal to their winter line. German troops struck sharply at Canadian units of the Eighth Army northwest of Vasto in the central Italian sector but were repulsed after a hard two-hour battle, the Allied command said today.

Throughout the mountainous inland sector the enemy was firing and dynamiting everything he could not carry with him to his powerful new gun-studded defense line. Smoke shrouded the horizon as the sizable cities of Castel di Sangro and Alfedena burned through the second day.

Reds Fall Back In Face of Nazi Counterdrive

Withdrawals Made West of Kiev; Gain Costly to Enemy

By Judson O'Quinn
London (Wednesday), Nov. 24 (AP).—The German counterattack in Russia, rising to new intensity, wrested several populated places from the Russians after hand-to-hand fighting and savage gun duels in which more than 100 German tanks were destroyed and 2000 Nazi soldiers were killed, Moscow announced today.

The Russians failed to locate the places they evacuated, but said the Germans were flinging large forces of tanks and infantry into their counterattacks in the Chernyakhov-Brusilov area of the northern Ukraine.

Here, where the Russians reach farthest west, and have retreated from Zhitomir, the Germans were smashing at the flank of the Soviet

Italy

The Italian campaign originated in some doubt and controversy. Since the Combined Chiefs were unable to agree where to make their offensive move after Sicily they instructed Eisenhower to set up two headquarters, each to plan a different invasion. Because Patton was occupied in Sicily, Eisenhower put Clark in charge of this planning. Whether the Allies eventually went to Sardinia and Corsica or to southern Italy, Clark would be the commander of the Allied forces involved.

On 17th July, a week after the Sicilian invasion, when it was obvious that Italian morale and resistance had seriously declined, Eisenhower and his principal subordinates discussed the idea of moving at once

Scylla to Charybdis; amphibious craft enter the water at the Straits of Messina to cross to the Italian mainland

across the strait of Messina to knock Italy out of the war. Although a thrust of this sort would have undoubtedly pushed Italy into surrender, the lack of Allied shipping and fighter air cover imposed restraints. After much soul-searching, together with strict calculations of tonnages and troops required, Eisenhower reluctantly conceded that no immediate move was possible. The Allies would have to wait until the completion of the Sicilian campaign to make another move.

While waiting, Eisenhower sought to shake Italian morale still further. Although Rome had thus far in the war been exempt from Allied bombardment because of its religious and historic monuments, Eisenhower authorized an air attack on Rome's railroad yards and on the airfields immediately south of the city.

On 19th July, 400 bombers dropped 1,000 tons of bombs on these targets and thereby showed the Italian government and people how close they were to defeat and bankruptcy.

Six days later, the Fascist Grand Council, in concert with the King, removed Mussolini from power. King Victor Emmanuel appointed Marshal Pietro Badoglio to be the new Premier. Although Badoglio pledged that Italy would continue the struggle beside the Germans, it became clear that Italy would try to get out of the war.

Eisenhower and his staff considered the possibility of invading Italy immediately upon their receipt of news that Mussolini had been removed. Again, the lack of shipping, planes, troops, and supplies curtailed a bold venture of this sort. There was nothing to do but await the end of the fighting in Sicily.

As for the Germans, they were concerned with the potential isolation of their forces fighting in Sicily and stationed in southern Italy. If Italy capitulated in conjunction with an Allied invasion, the German troops in the country would be trapped. To guarantee their safety, Hitler rushed military units into northern Italy and gradually began to occupy the country.

The Allies began to consider how they might best get Italy to the point of actual surrender. While Roosevelt and Churchill thought about the formal terms they might offer Italy to gain capitulation, Eisenhower was interested in an armistice from a purely military viewpoint. If he could turn the Italians against the Germans, the Allies could occupy the mainland without fighting. They would come into possession of Italian airfields, and they could release troops from the Mediterranean theater for the cross-Channel operation. In other words, an Italian surrender promised to save time and Allied lives.

When queried for his opinion, Eisenhower informed his superiors that he was concerned with military victory rather than with political ideology. He was willing to permit the King to retain his throne if that would convince the government to sue for peace. He suggested that continuous propaganda broadcasts be made to the Italian people in order to commend them and their King for ridding themselves of Mussolini and to urge them to come over on the Allied side against the Germans.

As Eisenhower worked out the details of what he would do if Badoglio asked for an armistice, Churchill and Roosevelt concluded that they would insist on the announced Allied policy toward the Axis, unconditional surrender. Eisenhower was more practical. Feeling that the Italian people wanted peace, he recognized that it might be impossible for the Italian government to make peace because of the presence of considerable numbers of German troops in the country.

On 17th August, the day the Sicilian campaign came to an end, Eisenhower learned that Giuseppe Castellano, a general officer in the Italian high command, had talked with the British ambassador in Madrid about an armistice. Castellano proposed

King Victor Emmanuel of Italy conferring decorations. The king acquiesced to Mussolini's removal from power

that if the Allies would land on the Italian mainland in force, thereby liberating the Italians from the Germans, Italy would join the Allies in the war against Germany.

By this time, Eisenhower had written out a few general conditions to govern the Italian surrender. These became known as the 'short terms.' At the same time, Roosevelt and Churchill and their political advisers formulated a set of more comprehensive conditions known as the 'long terms.'

In the interest of obtaining the Italian surrender and all the advantages this would bring, Eisenhower sent his Chief of Staff, Smith, and his G-2, Kenneth Strong, to Madrid to talk with Castellano. They were to try to convince him to accept the short terms enunciated by Eisenhower as the basis for an armistice, while making clear that Italy would later have to accept the economic, political, and financial conditions of the long terms.

Marshal Pietro Badoglio replaces Mussolini as Premier

Smith and Strong conversed with Castellano on 19th August. They gave him the short terms to take to Rome for the Badoglio government to study.

While Castellano was showing the short terms to the government in Rome, Eisenhower received from the Combined Chiefs of Staff the comprehensive surrender document known as the long terms. Forty-one paragraphs covered military, civil, social, economic, and political affairs. According to Macmillan, the document was 'a planner's dream and a general's nightmare.' It showed little awareness of what was clear to Eisenhower and his staff. The Italians were between the devil and the deep blue sea, between the imminent occupation of their country by the Germans and the imminent invasion of their country by the Allies.

By this time, another Italian emissary, this one named Giacomo Zanussi, also a general officer, had arrived in Lisbon and expressed the desire, through the British embassy, to come to terms with the Allies. Flown to Algiers to talk directly with Eisen-

Testing terrain for the infantry

hower, Zanussi said that the Italians wanted at least fifteen Allied divisions to land in Italy, preferably near Rome, and protect the government against the Germans.

This was manifestly impossible, not only because the Allies lacked a force of this size but also because the decision to invade Italy elsewhere had already been made.

If Eisenhower had the requisite means to land at Rome in force, seize the capital, and expel the Germans, he could manage the surrender without difficulty. Unfortunately, the landing ships and craft he had available could transport but three divisions to the mainland for an amphibious assault. The range of fighter aircraft based on Sicilian airfields permitted at most an invasion near, not Rome, but Naples, a hundred miles to the south.

The Italians had overestimated Allied strength in the Mediterranean area, and Eisenhower could hardly afford to let them see how weak the Allies actually were.

While Eisenhower and Zanussi were talking, Montgomery's Eighth Army crossed the strait of Messina on the morning of 3rd September, and took the first step in a three-pronged invasion of the Italian mainland.

Eisenhower tried to persuade Zanussi of the good faith of the Allied governments, their willingness to help the Italians surrender, even though it was impossible to accede to the demands for a landing at Rome in force. As a compromise, Eisenhower offered to send the 82nd Airborne Division to land at Rome in order to protect the Italian government from the Germans. But the airborne troops would parachute into the airfields around Rome only if the Italian army promised to protect the airfields from the Germans.

Zanussi returned to Rome to see about this.

On 4th September Eisenhower went to Sicily and watched Smith and Castellano sign the abbreviated armistice agreement. The Italians promised to sail their fleet from its home ports and surrender to Cunningham at Malta; and to announce their capitulation on the evening of 8th September a few hours before Clark's US Fifth Army landed at Salerno. Badoglio would acknowledge the surrender and Eisenhower the armistice over the radio at 6.30pm.

The final adjustments necessitated by the projected Rome operation were completed on 6th September. The 82nd Airborne Division, which was to have fulfilled a mission in Clark's invasion at Salerno was withdrawn from the Fifth Army so that it could prepare to fly to Rome.

As a last-minute precaution, Eisenhower sent two American officers, Maxwell Taylor and William T Gardiner, into Rome clandestinely to make the final arrangements with Badoglio regarding the protection of the airfields at Rome. Taylor and Gardiner went by PT boat to the Italian coast on the morning of 7th September, then by automobile to the capital.

They found the Italians apprehensive. The Allied forces, in the opinion of the government, were too small. The airborne operation and the Salerno invasion should be postponed.

The American officers managed to see Badoglio himself around midnight. They discovered that he was frightened. Taylor then sent a coded message to Eisenhower, reporting Badoglio's position. 'Due to changes in the situation . . . it is no longer possible [for Badoglio] to accept an immediate armistice.' Making peace with the Allies would only provoke the Germans into taking control over the country. Therefore, the 82nd Airborne drop at Rome, Taylor concluded, 'is no longer possible because of lack of [Italian] forces to guarantee the airfields.'

Knowing that the airborne troops were to take off from Sicily that evening (8th September), and fearing that the process of encoding and transmitting the message might prevent its receipt in time, Taylor sent two words that had been prearranged – 'situation innocuous' – recommending that the airborne operation be cancelled.

This reached the Sicilian airfields as the airborne troops were boarding their planes.

Meanwhile, Eisenhower had heard directly from Badoglio, who renounced the surrender. Enraged, Eisenhower radioed immediately to Badoglio:

'I intend to broadcast the existence of the armistice at the hour originally planned. If you or any part of your armed forces fail to cooperate as previously agreed I will publish to the world the full record of this affair . . . The sole hope of Italy is bound up in your adherence to that agreement . . . Plans have been made on the assumption that you were acting in good faith and we have been prepared to carry out future operations on that basis. Failure now on your part to carry out the full obligations to the signed agreement will have the most

German officers interrogate Italian officers in Rome after Marshal Badoglio's Armistice with the Allies in September 1943

serious consequences for your country. No future action of yours could then restore any confidence whatever in your good faith and consequently the dissolution of your government and nation would ensue.'

That evening, at 6.30, exactly on schedule, although he had received no further word from Badoglio, Eisenhower broadcast from Radio Algiers. He announced that the Italian government had surrendered unconditionally and that he had granted a military armistice. 'Italians who now act to help eject the German aggressor from Italian soil,' he concluded, 'will have the assistance and support of the United Nations.'

The point was that the Salerno invasion was terribly risky. Any help that the Italians could give would be prized. Clark had less than four divisions; the Germans had nearly twenty divisions in Italy, and they could rush reinforcements to Salerno far more quickly than the Allies.

At 7.45pm Badoglio's voice came over Radio Rome. He announced the Italian surrender.

Eisenhower's matchless negotiations, his firm stand had convinced the Italian government to abandon the Germans. The entire matter was hardly settled, for the long terms had yet to be attended to, but Eisenhower had given the Salerno invasion, one of the riskiest amphibious landings during the war, a better chance of success.

'I feel', Eisenhower radioed the Combined Chiefs on 9th September, 'that AVALANCHE' – the invasion at Salerno – 'will be a matter of touch and go for the next few days.' The major reason was the lack of landing craft to put another division ashore at once. 'We are in for some very tough fighting,' Eisenhower predicted.

But at least the Italians would not be opposing the British and American troops coming ashore. Neither would they, it would turn out, offer much help by moving against the Germans.

Southern Italy

Steaming into Salerno Bay ; an escort
lays a smoke-screen as cover for
landing-craft

The invasion of the mainland of Italy was a three-part operation. On 3rd September Montgomery's British Eighth Army moved across the strait of Messina into the toe of Italy against no opposition. On 9th September the British 1st Airborne Division, transported in warships, made an impromptu landing at Taranto, where Italian troops, happy to be out of the war, helped them come ashore. On the same day, at dawn, Clark's US Fifth Army, composed of a British corps and an American corps, met stiff German resistance on the beaches of Salerno.

The planning and preparations for Salerno had been a nightmare of complications. Firstly, because there was no firm decision at the Combined Chiefs' level on whether the Allies

would invade Sardinia and Corsica or the mainland of Italy, planning was tentative for a prolonged period of time. Secondly, the decision for southern Italy having been made rather late and on the basis of persuading the Badoglio government to surrender, there was no obviously suitable place for the Allies to land.

Rome, the immediate strategic objective, was simply too distant from Sicily; fighter planes flying from Sicilian airfields lacked the range to give the landing forces cover. Even Naples, a strategic objective because of its fine port, was too far away to permit adequate air cover. Salerno, at the outer edge of fighter range, was finally chosen even though the mountains ringing the beaches would·give the defenders a bird's-eye view of the landing.

Thirdly, landing at Salerno required the Allied forces subsequently to fight their way across the Sorrento mountain range, which was penetrated by two narrow passes easily defended. The 82nd Airborne Division was to have parachuted into the area to seize these passes, but the aborted attempt to send the division to Rome made it impossible to carry out this mission.

Furthermore the two British divisions and the single American division making the initial assault at Salerno were judged too slender a force to guarantee success.

It was for these reasons that the Italian surrender loomed so large in the Allied calculation. Yet while Clark's men were on their way to Salerno, the Germans were moving to take control of Rome and to capture the King and his government.

Despite the hazards of Salerno, the Allies had hope of quick success because of a particular intelligence estimate. Allied intelligence officers had discovered that Hitler had no intention of holding southern Italy in the event of an Allied invasion. More concerned about extricating the German divisions stationed in

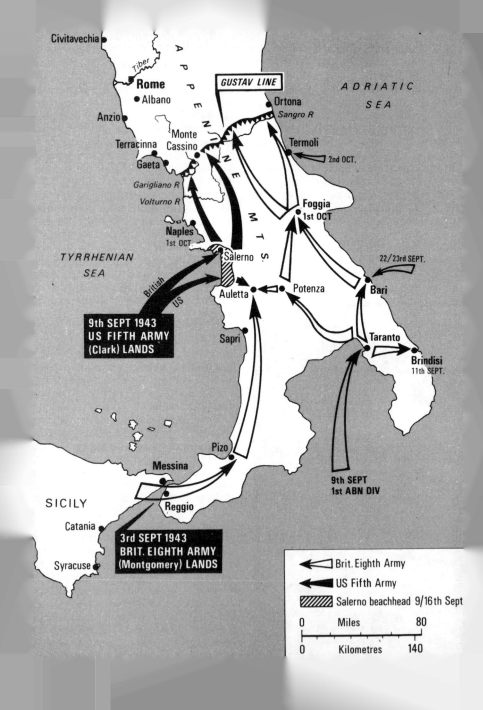

Civitavechia

Tiber

Rome
● Albano

Anzio

Terracinna

Gaeta

Monte
Cassino

Garigliano R

Volturno R

A P P E N I N E

M T S.

GUSTAV LINE

Ortona
Sangro R

Termoli

← 2nd OCT.

A D R I A T I C
S E A

Foggia
1st OCT

Naples
1st OCT.

T Y R R H E N I A N
S E A

Salerno

Auletta

Potenza

Bari

22/23rd SEPT.

British

US

**9th SEPT 1943
US FIFTH ARMY
(Clark) LANDS**

Sapri

Taranto

Brindisi
11th SEPT.

Pizo

**9th SEPT
1st ABN DIV**

Messina

Reggio

SICILY

Catania

Syracuse

**3rd SEPT 1943
BRIT. EIGHTH ARMY
(Montgomery) LANDS**

← Brit. Eighth Army

← US Fifth Army

▨ Salerno beachhead 9/16th Sept

0   Miles   80

0   Kilometres   140

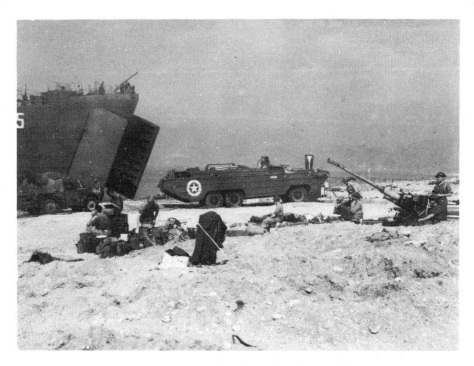

Above : Defensive preparations at Red Beach, Salerno
Below : Mortar shells pound the beach and forming-up areas

the south of Italy, Hitler ordered his Commander-in-Chief, Albert Kesselring, to fight the Allies only to the extent of insuring the safe withdrawal of two divisions in the toe, a third in the Foggia area, and several others south of Rome.

If the Germans followed this strategy and moved north, first to Rome, then to a defensive position in the northern Apennines, the Allies could come into possession of most of the country on the cheap. With the magnificent port of Naples, the splendid airfields around Foggia, and the psychologically important capital of Rome in their hands, they could then decide whether to pursue the Germans to the Alps, to cross the Adriatic and invade the Balkans, to turn westward toward southern France, or to halt operations and make available significant resources to the forces being

An unhappy Kesselring has the task of extricating the German divisions in southern Italy

Kesselring orders bridges to be destroyed to hinder the Allies' advance

built up for a cross-Channel offensive.

But first Clark's Fifth Army had to get ashore at Salerno. And as Eisenhower had anticipated, the combat on the beaches and in the foothills just behind was fierce. Kesselring had his two divisions in the toe demolish roads, bridges, and culverts to hold up Montgomery's advance; he then moved them to the Salerno battlefield. He also sent some local reinforcements to the scene of action from the Naples area.

With Clark unable to augment his landing forces as quickly as the Germans could bolster theirs, the struggle for the beachhead soon turned against the Allies. On 12th September the Germans launched a counterattack that came within a hair of driving to the water's edge and splitting the British and American sectors. Clark began to think seriously of evacuating the Americans from

A destroyer off Salerno makes smoke during a 'red alert'

their beaches in order to reinforce the British, or of withdrawing the British in order to reinforce the Americans. Meanwhile, he ordered his troops to stand and fight.

In order to help Clark retain the foothold his men had clawed on the beaches, Eisenhower ordered Tedder to use heavy or strategic bombers in a tactical rôle. The airmen were unhappy to divert their heavy bombers from their strategic missions of hitting industrial and transportation targets far in the enemy rear, but under Eisenhower's instructions, they sent the aircraft over the Salerno plain to plaster German troop concentrations and traffic.

Eisenhower also ordered Cunningham to have his naval commanders move their warships closer to shore and to step up their shelling. The naval authorities were reluctant to expose their ships to the increased

dangers of working close to land, but under Eisenhower's insistence, they did so and gave Clark invaluable support.

With the ground troops fighting a magnificent defensive action and the air and naval forces giving excellent help, the battle swung to the favor of the Allies. The Germans began to withdraw.

This was no clearcut Allied victory. Kesselring had ordered his troops to withdraw in consonance with Hitler's strategy. Having prevented his troops in the south from being trapped, Kesselring began to move slowly to the north, giving ground grudgingly and inflicting relatively high casualties on the Allies who advanced doggedly against him.

The Salerno battle was over on 20th September and ten days later Clark's troops marched into Naples and began rehabilitating the port that the Germans had demolished before departing. At the same time, Montgomery's men moved across the

General Mark Clark watches his armor

rugged country in the south and captured the Foggia airfields.

The Italian armed forces had simply vanished. The units dissolved, and the men went home. The military had offered no help to the Allied invaders. In addition, the king and the government had fled from Rome to avoid capture by Kesselring's forces and were in Bari. What then was to be done to implement the armistice?

Eisenhower informed the Combined Chiefs of Staff that he saw only two alternatives. The Allies could accept and strengthen the Italian government and grant Italy the status of a co-belligerent to make possible Italian participation in the war against Germany. Or the Allies could sweep the Badoglio government aside and set up an Allied military government, which meant a heavy commitment in military personnel. He strongly favored the first alternative.

The Allied leaders acted upon Eisenhower's suggestion and decided to let the Italians fight beside the Allies if the Badoglio government declared war on Germany and promised to hold elections after the war in order to let the people decide the form of government they wished.

Badoglio wanted to wait to declare war until after the Allies took Rome.

Eisenhower would have none of that. He said that the government would have to declare war at once. He also exerted pressure to have Badoglio change some of the members of his government to give it an anti-Fascist character.

In the belief that the Allies would soon enter Rome and in the hope that Italian troops would accompany the Allies into the Eternal City, Badoglio accepted Eisenhower's conditions. Aboard the British battleship *Nelson* at Malta Eisenhower and Badgolio met on 29th September. Badgolio signed the long terms, which included the promise of postwar elections. Two weeks later the government declared

Marshal Badoglio reads Italy's declaration of war against Germany in the watchful presence of Brigadier-General Maxwell D Taylor

war on Germany.

Now Eisenhower would have to initiate an effort to re-form the dissolved Italian military units, rearm and re-equip them, and retrain them to fight alongside the Allies. Although he wished to use Italian troops to guard the lines of communication and logistical installations, he had to accede to Italian requests for a share in the glory. He would have to accept combat troops. In November, a hurriedly retrained Italian brigade joined the Allied troops on the front, and as the campaign progressed, as more units were reconstituted, they would take a larger part in the fighting.

The Allied strategy in southern Italy as enunciated by Eisenhower was to keep in contact with the Germans, who were withdrawing slowly, keep them off balance and prevent them from launching a spoiling counterattack, and seize Rome with its political prestige and its airfields.

So long as the Germans continued to implement Hitler's strategy of giving up southern Italy, the major problem for the Allied armies was to overcome the extreme difficulties of the terrain that facilitated the German defense.

In October, Allied intelligence noted signs of an alteration in the German strategy. Kesselring's success at Salerno and his subsequent slow withdrawal from the Sorrento range, from Naples and Foggia, and from the Volturno – during which he inflicted heavy casualties on the advancing Allied troops – prompted Hitler to change his mind. He decided to accept Kesselring's recommendation that the Germans stand and fight below Rome,

Despite bombing of German defenses the Allies suffer heavily crossing the Volturno

where the narrowness of the Italian peninsula and the mountainous terrain would be most advantageous to a defensive effort.

By November, the Germans had constructed three major lines of defense. The Barbara Line was in reality a strong outpost, and the Bernhard Line was a strongly fortified series of positions – the Allies called them both the Winter Line. The third was the formidable Gustav Line, which was anchored on the Garigliano and Rapido Rivers and the towering height of Monte Cassino in the western part of the peninsula, on the Sangro River in the east.

As the Allies moved against these positions tenaciously held by the Germans, progress slowed and casualties rose. With the cheerless prospect of fighting a frontal war in well defined corridors of advance through the mountains – highly favorable to defensive rather than offensive operations – Eisenhower began to search for a more painless way of getting to Rome. 'We are looking every minute,' he informed Marshall, 'for a chance to utilize our air and naval power to turn the enemy positions and place him at a disadvantage.'

What he was talking about was the possibility of going around the German defenses by a waterborne expedition or over them by an airborne venture. Since the terrain was unsuitable for airborne operations, Eisenhower increasingly became persuaded that the answer to the need for quicker movement up the boot of Italy was by amphibious means.

On 31st October, he therefore asked the Combined Chiefs for permission to keep sixty-eight landing ships in the theater until 5th January, three weeks beyond their scheduled departure for the United Kingdom, where they would be added to the cross-Channel buildup. If he could retain these ships, he could plan an amphibious operation designed to get the Allies quickly to Rome.

Although there was some question

that delaying the departure of this large number of landing ships might have an adverse affect on the preparations of what was already being called OVERLORD, the Combined Chiefs on 5th November gave Eisenhower the permission he sought. Brooke told Alexander privately that he was sure that the theater could hold the ships for a longer time, but he had no authority to make a firm promise. Even so, Clark believed that he could mount and stage a landing at Anzio in the approved time frame.

On this basis, on 8th November, Eisenhower authorized and Alexander issued a plan for what became known as Operation SHINGLE, a landing at Anzio, twenty miles below Rome. The object was to go around the Barnhard and Gustav Lines by sea and land in the enemy's rear, thereby causing the Germans to pull back from Monte Cassino in order to protect their route of withdrawal to Rome.

Unfortunately, it was obvious to all the Allied commanders that Clark's Fifth Army needed to get farther up the peninsula, closer to Anzio, so that the forces on the main front could make a quick link-up with the forces brought ashore and holding an Anzio beachhead. The stubborn German defense, the onset of bad winter weather, the growing exhaustion of the Allied troops, and the extremely difficult terrain all conspired to indicate that the Allied advance to the north was bogging down. Not only Clark's offensive west of the Apennines, but Montgomery's in the east came virtually to a halt.

Eisenhower called off Alexander's Rome operation. Perhaps, he told his 'subordinate commanders, he could get his superiors to allow him to retain the landing ships beyond 5th January. On 24th November Eisenhower flew to Cairo to attend meetings of the Allied leaders and of the Combined Chiefs of Staff. He outlined his accomplishments and problems in Italy and indicated that he required more landing craft in order to get to

Rome.

The question remained unresolved until December, when Churchill managed to secure Roosevelt's acquiescence to letting the landing ships remain in the Mediterranean theater until 15th February; and with that Anzio became feasible. The main front though, where the troops – held back by rain and snow in the mountains – were inching through the awesome German defenses, was not much closer to the intended landing site at Anzio.

By then, Eisenhower was at the point of departing the Mediterranean area for another assignment. Among his last duties as Supreme Allied Commander, Mediterranean theater, he prepared an outline plan for an invasion of southern France, this to be launched in 1944, simultaneously with OVERLORD. He also supervised, but without meddling, the final planning for the Anzio operation.

On the last day of 1943, Eisenhower left the Mediterranean and went to

Roosevelt and Eisenhower travel together to a conference

Washington for consultations and a rest. For he had been chosen to lead the cross-Channel attack.

During his year in command of the Allied forces in the Mediterranean area, he had been responsible for many achievements. He had engineered the invasion of North Africa, brought the French into the war on the Allied side, cleared the northern shore of Africa, invaded and conquered Sicily, brought about the surrender of Italy, and started the campaign on the Italian mainland. With a shortage of resources in men and materials, he had initiated and maintained a momentum that had taken the Allied forces onto the European continent. Now he would take command of what was regarded as the climactic operation against Germany, the invasion of north-west Europe, this to be followed by a direct thrust to the heart of the enemy territory.

79

'Overlord'

The Normandy beaches feel the weight
of the enormous supplies build-up

Since the summer of 1943, a planning group headed by Sir Frederick Morgan had been drawing the blueprint for OVERLORD. Although he was Chief of Staff to the Supreme Allied Commander (COSSAC), Morgan was in an awkward position because no commander had been chosen. Restricted to the planning function, Morgan lacked the authority to request or to requisition the units and *matériel* he saw as being necessary for a successful invasion.

By the end of 1943, the decision to appoint a commander could no longer be deferred. Although the selection of a supreme Allied commander was within the prerogatives of the Combined Chiefs of Staff, they preferred to let Churchill and Roosevelt make

that decision. Since the Americans would ultimately give the preponderant contribution in men and *matériel* to the invasion and subsequent campaigns, actually twice the amount contributed by the British, the choice rested with Roosevelt.

Earlier, when it had appeared that the British and American participation would be nearly equal, Churchill had talked about appointing Brooke to be the supreme Allied commander. Brooke was highly eligible. He was experienced, and he had sufficient prestige to command the respect and the cheerful obedience of subordinates. But when it became obvious that the extent of the American effort would overshadow that of the British, Brooke stepped aside, although he was personally disappointed.

The only individual who equalled Brooke in personal prestige and experience was Marshall, who was the obvious choice of all. Marshall himself had been responsible for the original concept of the invasion – as early as the spring of 1942 he had had Eisenhower, who was then working in his office, draw a plan for an invasion of France. Marshall also had been the most outspoken advocate of the direct power thrust across the Channel and into the heart of Germany.

This seemed to be the sensible thing to do, name Marshall to head the Allied invasion and have Eisenhower replace him in Washington as the US Army Chief of Staff. Yet there was much reluctance to move Marshall from Washington, where he was the central figure in the deliberations of the Joint Chiefs of Staff and of the Combined Chiefs. The strongest exponent of global coordination, Marshall was also Roosevelt's most trusted military adviser. Although Roosevelt knew that Marshall would be disappointed if he were not given the assignment, he told him he would be unable to sleep securely if Marshall were out

Above: Lieutenant-General F E Morgan heads the planning group for OVERLORD
Below: General George C Marshall, with Eisenhower in North Africa. Roosevelt would not release him from Washington to take command of the invasion

of Washington.

Roosevelt probably made up his mind to select Eisenhower as the OVERLORD commander during the Cairo conference. He asked Churchill what his reaction was, and Churchill said that he would be delighted to have Eisenhower in command. When the two leaders met with Stalin at Yalta, Roosevelt told the Russian that Eisenhower would command the invasion.

After the Cairo and Yalta conferences, Roosevelt stopped in Tunis on his way back to Washington. Eisenhower flew from Algiers to meet him. As the two men were travelling in Eisenhower's car from the airport to the city, Roosevelt nonchalantly said, 'Well, Ike, you are going to command OVERLORD.'

Eisenhower was genuinely surprised, for he expected Marshall to lead the invasion.

In actuality, there was no more logical choice for the task than Eisenhower. In terms of experience and demonstrated ability, as well

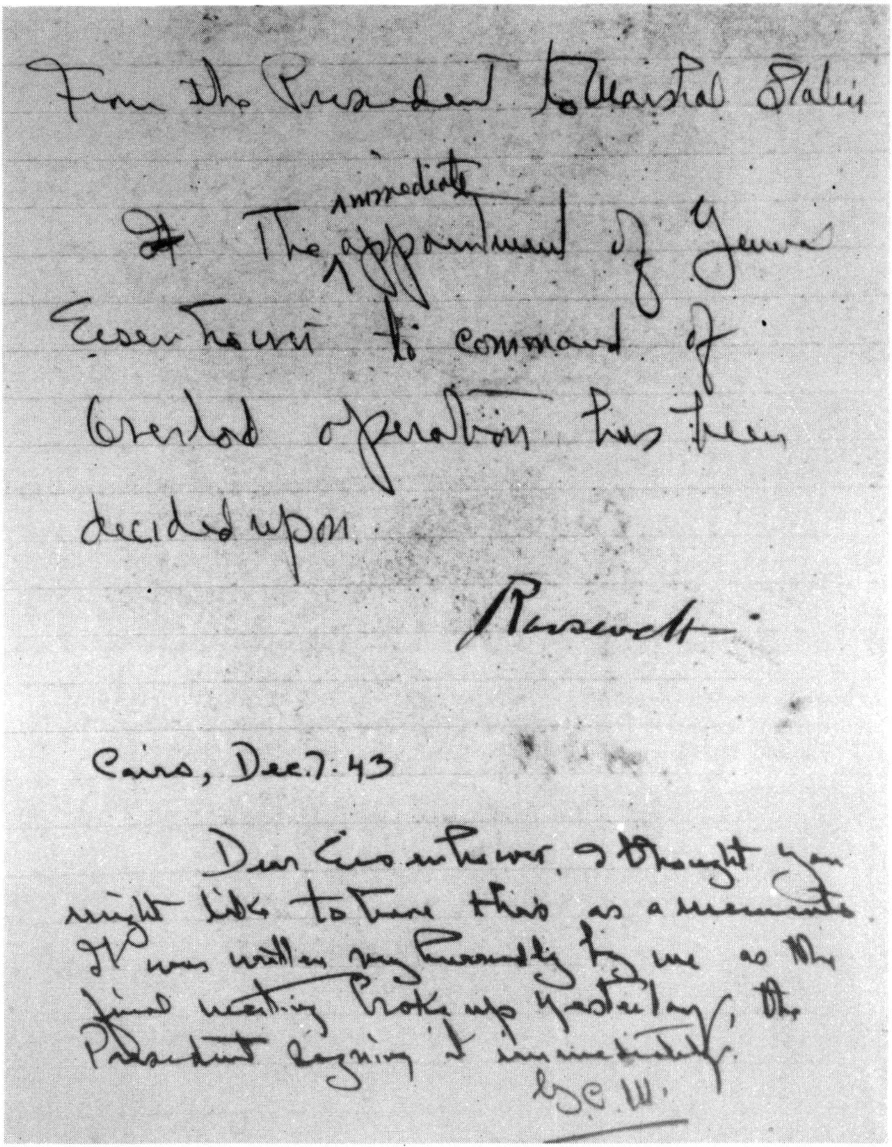

From the President to Marshal Stalin

The immediate appointment of General Eisenhower to command of Overlord operation has been decided upon.

Roosevelt

Cairo, Dec.7.43

Dear Eisenhower, I thought you might like to have this as a memento. It was written very hurriedly by me as the final meeting broke up yesterday, the President signing it immediately.

bye W.

as in terms of results attained, no one else could bring such expertise to the job of managing and directing a huge and complex coalition effort.

Eisenhower had come far in the year and a half since he had been named, with some misgiving, to take charge of TORCH.

To assist him carry out the invasion and campaign of north-west Europe,

Marshall's original draft of the decision to appoint Eisenhower as OVERLORD commander, signed by the President

Eisenhower formed the Supreme Headquarters, Allied Expeditionary Force (SHAEF). It was very much like AFHQ in form, basically American in structure, yet with integrated Anglo-American staff sections.

Above : Patton and Omar Bradley, heading respectively Third and First US Armies, return from visiting the fronts. *Below :* Eisenhower would have preferred Alexander to command the British ground forces ; Churchill chose Montgomery

Above left : Carl Spaatz is given command of US strategic bombers. *Above right :* Admiral Sir Bertram Home Ramsay, commander of the invasion fleet
Below right : Air Chief Marshal Sir Trafford Leigh-Mallory wishes to have the operation postponed owing to unfavorable weather

Bedell Smith went with Eisenhower to be Chief of Staff. Tedder was appointed deputy supreme Allied commander. Carl Spaatz headed the American strategic bombers. Bradley was in command of the US First Army, also the US 1st Army Group. Patton was to command the US Third Army. Although Eisenhower planned for Alexander to command the British ground troops, Churchill preferred to leave him in the Mediterranean and chose, instead, Montgomery.

Rounding out the top commanders for the invasion were Sir Trafford Leigh-Mallory, who would head the Allied Expeditionary Air Forces, those working to soften up the enemy defenses. Sir Henry Ramsay would be the Allied naval commander, responsible for transporting the troops across the Channel and supporting them when they went ashore.

To replace Eisenhower himself as Supreme Allied Commander, Mediterranean theater, Churchill appointed H Maitland Wilson, an officer who had commanded the British in the Middle East. To command the American contingents in the Mediterranean and to be the senior American officer in that area, Jacob L Devers was brought to Algiers from London, where he had been in command of the American buildup for OVERLORD.

The big job of OVERLORD in execution was to deposit troops ashore who would stay and be reinforced for the subsequent thrust towards Germany. The Pas de Calais, across the Channel at its narrowest part, was the obvious landing site; near Antwerp, one of the great ports of Europe, it opened to the most direct path to Germany. But the German defenses were naturally strongest in the Pas de Calais as they were expecting a crossing there.

To disrupt their expectations, the Allies would land in Normandy, on the shore of the Bay of the Seine. After taking the Cotentin peninsula, which would give them the port of Cherbourg, the Allies would move from Caen across the Falaise plain, which would offer them flat ground for airfields, and directly toward Paris. Once at the Seine River and holding the lodgment area, which was defined by the Seine and the Loire rivers, the Allies would build up their invasion forces and mount the attack toward Germany. That was the plan in outline.

But first Eisenhower would have to get his men across the water and sieze and enlarge the beachhead into the proportions of the lodgment area. The initial landings would be made at low tide so that the mined and underwater obstacles erected by the Germans all along the Channel beaches would be uncovered. The sea crossings would be made during the hours of darkness but on a night with some moon so that paratroopers and glidermen would have sufficient light for their landings. Until the port of Cherbourg could be siezed, artificial harbors and breakwaters were to be towed across the Channel and set up off the invasion beaches in order to provide facilities for unloading.

After spending the first two weeks of January 1944 in the United States, Eisenhower went to London and studied the COSSAC plan in detail. His preliminary reading of Morgan's OVERLORD plan convinced him, together with Montgomery and Smith, that the initial assault had to be widened and strengthened. Three divisions, to which Morgan had been limited because of shortages in landing craft, were insufficient in Eisenhower's opinion to ensure success.

In order to obtain more landing craft, D-day was postponed from May to 5th June. This would give manufacturers in the United States and Britain more time to produce the vessels needed. Furthermore, since the Anzio landings were scheduled and would require the retention of landing ships in the Mediterranean, perhaps the invasion of southern France, codenamed ANVIL, could be scratched.

Allied plans for further landings in Europe

Eisenhower wanted ANVIL. He was less interested in Anzio, which he regarded as a hazardous operation hardly necessary in what had already become a subsidiary front. He saw a southern France operation as a far more useful endeavor, for it would fashion a giant pincer against the Germans in Normandy, sticking into their flank and impelling them to relinquish their hold over all of France; it would give the Allies the port of Marseilles which could receive American divisions and materials coming directly from the United States for use in Europe; it would give the French forces in North Africa which were being re-equipped and retrained the best place for their active employment in battle.

Eisenhower was therefore inclined to take landing craft from the Mediterranean and use them against southern France.

Churchill insisted on Anzio. Since Eisenhower continued to favor ANVIL, a compromise was reached. The landings in southern France were postponed. Instead of occurring simultaneously with OVERLORD, ANVIL would be delayed until the Allies took Rome. Then landing craft and ships could be used to transport some forces from Italy to southern France.

As Eisenhower began to tune up the huge and ponderous invasion machine during the early months of 1944, doubts and hesitations affected some of his important subordinates. For example, three airborne divisions were to drop into Normandy several hours ahead of the amphibious assault. Their principal task was to block the Germans from moving in against the amphibious forces during the first few hours of the invasion when amphibiously transported ground troops were at their most vulnerable. Conversely, the paratroopers were to secure the exits from the landing beaches and allow the soldiers coming ashore from boats to move away from the beaches and into the interior.

The 6th British Airborne Division was to drop on the left of the invasion and anchor the front near the mouth of the Orne River. The 82nd and 101st US Divisions were to drop on the right of the invasion front and anchor that end of the line in the Contentin peninsula.

Leigh Mallory became intensely concerned over the presence of strong German troops in precisely those places where the 101st and 82nd were to jump. He predicted that if Eisenhower permitted the landings to go as scheduled, the casualties in the 101st would be enormous, as high as seventy per cent of the unit.

After studying the question, Eisenhower decided that the airborne operations were absolutely necessary. He was convinced that the casualties would be far less than the proportion forecast by Leigh Mallory.

Yet his anxiety led him to spend part of the last day before the invasion with these troops. He was heartened to see them in such good spirits. They assured him they were ready to go and would do the job.

After the fact, Eisenhower was proved to have been right. The airborne casualties were light, and the paratroopers and glidermen contributed handsomely to the success of the amphibious assault.

Leigh Mallory, a few days after the invasion, apologized for having added to the tremendous cares and strains that afflicted Eisenhower on the eve of the operation.

The most meticulously prepared large-scale amphibious operation ever attempted, OVERLORD was ready to go when the weather unexpectedly deteriorated. Tides and phases of the moon were predictable, but not storms. As the wind picked up speed, as rain came thundering in over western Europe, it seemed as though high seas and overcast skies would make the invasion impossible. Aircraft would be unable to carry out their last-minute missions. Small ships would founder in the heavy seas and be unable to reach their predetermined beaches. Seasick soldiers would be in no condition to fight.

Yet if OVERLORD were postponed until the weather cleared, it would be several weeks before the landings could be rescheduled to coincide with the favorable tides and the moon. By then, much of the summer, the best time of the year for campaigning, would have gone.

On the evening of 3rd June, Eisenhower drove to Ramsay's headquarters near Portsmouth, where he would remain during the critical hours and first few days of the invasion. He learned from his chief meteorologist that a high pressure system was moving out, followed by a low pressure system that would bring bad weather.

At 4.30am, on 4th June, the day before the scheduled crossing, the meteorologists said that the sea conditions would be somewhat better than originally expected but that the overcast would prevent the air forces from functioning properly.

Later that day the meteorologists predicted that the sea conditions would improve but still make naval support inefficient and might interfere with the handling of the small boats.

Eisenhower asked his principal subordinates what they believed ought to be done. Montgomery said he wanted to go anyway. Tedder and Leigh Mallory favored postponing the operation. Ramsay was neutral.

After listening, Eisenhower summed up the crux of the problem. The ground forces, he said, were not overwhelmingly powerful. The operation was feasible only if the Allies could use their air superiority. Without that advantage, the landings would to too risky. On that basis, he decided to postpone the landings for twenty-four hours.

Word was immediately sent to the ships, which sailed back to their ports, refueled, and prepared to move out again on the following day.

On the evening of 4th June, the wind and the rain rattled the windows of Southwick House, where Eisenhower had established his headquarters. About 0930 the chief meteorologist gave a weather report. He announced a break. The rain, he said, would stop in a few hours, and the winds would moderate. Bombers and fighter planes would be able to operate, although they would be hampered by clouds.

With his subordinates, Eisenhower discussed whether to let the invasion go on 6th June. He himself wished to put off the final decision until the following morning. But Ramsay pointed out that the fleet had to know within the next half hour in the event that a positive decision was made. A negative decision could later stop the invasion, but if there was to be an invasion on the 6th, it would have to start that evening or the 4th. Otherwise, a forty-eight hour delay would be necessary, and on 8th June, the tidal conditions would be wrong. The next opportunity would occur on 19th June.

Lonely and isolated for the moment, Eisenhower made the decision. At 0945, he said, 'I am quite positive that the order must be given.'

He meant that the invasion was on. But there was still time to halt the massive machinery of the landings early on the following morning.

More than 5,000 ships began to move toward France.

After a night of fitful sleep, Eisenhower attended what would be the final pre-invasion conference early on 5th June. The wind still beat down in hurricane gusts, and the rain seemed to be driving horizontally. But as the meteorologist was talking, the sky began to clear, and the rain slackened off.

Eisenhower asked everyone to give his opinion on whether the invasion was practical in these weather conditions. After everyone had spoken, there was silence while the chief made up his mind.

Making for France; more than 5,000 ships comprise the invasion fleet

Eisenhower thought for a moment, then said clearly, though quietly, 'OK, let's go.'

Having given the word, he was from that point on for several days powerless to make any changes. For better or for worse, his decision had turned on the invasion, and now it had to go.

During that day of relative inactivity, Eisenhower scratched a few lines on a scrap of paper and put it into his wallet.

'Our landings in the Cherbourg-Havre area have failed to gain a satisfactory foothold and I have withdrawn the troops. My decision to attack at this time and place was based upon the best information available. The troops, the air and the navy did all that bravery and devotion to duty could do. If any blame or fault attaches to the attempt it is mine alone.'

A month later, when the invasion had become history, Eisenhower found the note and showed it to his aide. He confessed that he had written similar notes before every amphibious operation that he had commanded.

Because of the bad weather immediately preceding OVERLORD, the Germans were completely surprised. They had believed that an invasion would be impossible. For that reason, several division commanders responsible for defending parts of the shoreline were away attending a war game conference. Rommel, who commanded the troops manning the supposedly impregnable Atlantic Wall, was off to Germany to celebrate his wife's birthday and to visit Hitler. The Allied deception plan, an elaborate hoax named FORTITUDE, made the Germans feel that the main invasion would come at the Pas de Calais. Allied naval and air bombardments cut telephone and telegraph lines.

As a consequence, the German reaction to the landings was at first con-

Above: Omaha Beach, where there is determined opposition. Elsewhere the defenders are caught off guard and initial resistance is light
Below: German troops and laborers rounded up in the early stages

fused and uncoordinated. Only at Omaha Beach did the invaders have real difficulties, for there they ran directly into a German division that Allied intelligence officers had failed to locate until too late to change the landing plan.

By the end of 6th June, it was obvious that the first day of the operation had ended in success. Even at Omaha, the troops were firmly ashore. At a cost of 2,500 casualties, the Allies had more than 23,000 airborne troops, plus 57,000 American and 75,000 British and Canadian troops in France. They had broken through Rommel's Atlantic Wall.

Impatient to see for himself what was happening, to be closer to the scene of action, Eisenhower crossed the Channel in a minelayer on 7th June. He met with Bradley and discussed the situation. The only influence he exerted on the battle was to order Bradley to have two American divisions move towards each other and link up at Carentan in order to provide a solid, continuous front.

Leaving the day-to-day decisions to Montgomery, Bradley, and his other subordinates, Eisenhower spent the first week of the Normandy invasion holding press conferences, answering messages of congratulation, meeting with Churchill and De Gaulle, gathering incoming information, urging his subordinates to redouble their efforts, attending a long conference dealing with invasion currency, and sending a message of congratulation to the Russians who had just launched their major offensive in the Leningrad area.

On 10th June, Marshall and the two other members of the American Joint Chiefs of Staff, Ernest J King and H H Arnold, arrived in London. Eisenhower discussed a variety of subjects with Marshall, including promotions for the higher-ranking officers, decorations, and shipping schedules. Two days later, they all went across the Channel in a destroyer, stepped ashore on Omaha Beach, and spent the better part of the day conferring with Brad-

ley and other commanders.

Impressed with the efficiency of the operation that Eisenhower had masterminded, Marshall sent Roosevelt a message: 'Eisenhower and his staff are cool and confident, carrying out an affair of incredible magnitude and complication with superlative efficiency.'

Eisenhower had overcome still another challenge, probably his greatest. Imperturbable in command, he had succeeded in carrying out the most dramatic event of the Second World War, OVERLORD, which would

serve to illustrate the extent of his capacity as a professional soldier. What Churchill called 'the most difficult and complicated operation that has ever taken place' had been an unqualified success.

There was one more indication of how right Eisenhower had been to postpone the invasion for one day but no longer. On 19th June, a severe storm struck the French coast. It destroyed one of the two artificial harbors and brought unloading operations to a halt. Had Eisenhower delayed the invasion beyond 6th June,

14th June 1944; US Army and Navy chiefs in Normandy. From the left: Arnold, Eisenhower, Marshall, Bradley and King

he would have had to execute it on the 19th; he would thus have run into the worst weather encountered in the Channel in twenty years. His gamble, his estimate of the situation and of the innumerable factors that played a role in the success or failure of a venture that had perhaps the most important effect on winning the war, had proved to be correct.

Normandy

US infantry move into the well defended
bocage

The Normandy campaign beyond the invasion beaches lasted through the summer of 1944. It started in frustration and ended in exultation. In little more than three months, the Allies surged from the landing beaches across France to the German border.

Yet the beginning of that campaign was marked by disagreement and anxiety. Eisenhower, the Supreme Allied Commander, wanted to push hard to keep the Germans off balance. Montgomery, the Allied ground commander temporarily for the initial few months, was exasperatingly slow in the conduct of his operations. He sought balance in his tactical dispositions and used the two armies directly under him – Bradley's First US and Miles C Dempsey's Second

British – with caution.

The two commanders would be at odds over strategy and tactics, the proper method of defeating the enemy. In the end they both succeeded, but at considerable cost to their personal friendship. If personal relations were relatively unimportant when compared to the task of overcoming the Germans, the coalition nevertheless underwent strains and stresses.

Never before had Eisenhower had to exert so much self-restraint and patience with respect to a major subordinate. Whereas Eisenhower preferred the direct attack all along the line, Montgomery guarded his strength and operated slowly. In large part both policies reflected the differences in resources available to the two countries. The United States because of its industrial might and large manpower reservoir, wished to overpower the enemy, whereas the British, with restricted material and manpower, sought to conserve forces and equipment.

The divergence of thought and approach to the problem of defeating the Germans became apparent immediately after the invasion.

The tremendous amount of study and effort bent toward getting Allied troops ashore in Normandy prevented a comparable endeavor regarding the ground immediately inland. As a consequence, few commanders appreciated the difficulties of the hedgerow country. No special training had been instituted to overcome the natural obstacles of that region. No equipment had been designed to help the troops forward.

The major obstacles were hedgerows, half fence, half wall. Out of a base of earth anywhere from one to four feet in height and several feet thick grew vines, bushes, and trees. Property demarcations and protection for cattle against the winds blowing in from the sea, hedgerows cut the terrain of Normandy into tiny fields. They were excellent natural fortifications, and the German defenders

Bradley, Montgomery and Dempsey. Eisenhower finds the Allied ground commander's excessive caution exasperating

dug positions into the base of the hedgerows, usually at the corners. From there they were able to dominate a field with a single machine gun.

As a consequence, the Germans kept the Allies close to the landing beaches and restricted to a small beachhead. Since Eisenhower's two armies were unable to start a war of movement, held as they were to their initial foothold, he began to have nightmares that the campign might degenerate into the static fighting reminiscent of the trench warfare in the First World War.

This was exactly what Hitler wanted. He wished to prevent the motorized and mechanized Allied forces from breaking out of their beachhead and instituting the kind of war – *blitzkrieg* – that the Germans

had fashioned in Poland and France in 1939 and 1940.

To the attackers, advancing through the hedgerow country meant reducing each hedgerow in turn, and this required meticulous, slow, and painful progress by the small units, the platoons, at most the companies. To conquer a field meant setting up a small, full-scale operation. Once the attack penetrated a hedgerow line, there was another a few hundred feet ahead where the whole process had to be repeated.

Although all the Allied troops faced hedgerows in June and July, the Americans operating on the right of the front had by far the worse terrain. The British and Canadians on the left, once they moved several miles inland from the beaches, would enter relatively flat country, the Caen-Falaise plain.

In mid-May, a month before the invasion, Montgomery had presented a lecture to the senior commanders about to execute OVERLORD. Out-

Above : The *bocage* is perfect terrain for defence – advance is slow
Below : In the region of Caen a Sherman tank races to join the conflict

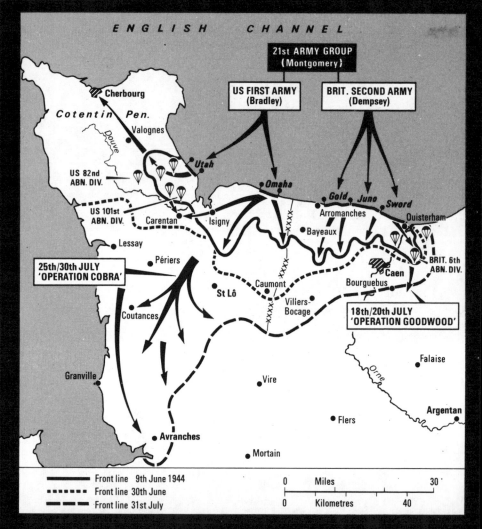

ENGLISH CHANNEL

21st ARMY GROUP (Montgomery)

US FIRST ARMY (Bradley)

BRIT. SECOND ARMY (Dempsey)

Cherbourg

Cotentin Pen.

Valognes

Douve

US 82nd ABN. DIV.

Utah

US 101st ABN. DIV.

Carentan

Isigny

Omaha

Gold *Juno* *Sword*

Arromanches

Ouisterham

Bayeaux

BRIT. 6th ABN. DIV.

Lessay

Périers

25th/30th JULY 'OPERATION COBRA'

St Lô

Caumont

Caen

Bourguebus

Villers-Bocage

18th/20th JULY 'OPERATION GOODWOOD'

Coutances

Falaise

Granville

Vire

Orne

Argentan

Flers

Avranches

Mortain

Front line 9th June 1944
Front line 30th June
Front line 31st July

0   Miles   30

0   Kilometres   40

6th June (D-Day) to 31st July

lining his plans, he said he expected to capture Caen on the first day of the invasion, then drive immediately inland toward Falaise on the way to Paris.

Everyone was pleased. The Caen-Falaise plain, the direct route to the French capital, offered ground suitable for tanks in armored warfare and for airfields on which to base close support planes. The implication was that this was where Montgomery planned to make his main effort. If the British and Canadian troops drove through Caen, they would pull the Americans through the worst of the hedgerow country.

The campaign beyond the invasion proceeded somewhat differently. After the troops landing on the five invasion beaches linked up and formed a solid beachhead, the Americans turned to the tip of the Cotentin peninsula in order to take Cherbourg, a port deemed vital for unloading the supplies and men required for the subsequent development of the campaign.

Destruction of a German pillbox during the advance on Cherbourg

On the last day of June, three weeks after the invasion, the Americans seized Cherbourg. The British and Canadians had yet to enter Caen.

Despite Montgomery's earlier intention to take Caen on D-day, he now rationalized his failure to do so by announcing that he had never cared specifically about Caen. 'My general policy,' he announced, 'is to pull the enemy on to the [British] Second Army so as to make it the easier for the [US] First Army to expand and extend the quicker.'

Actually, there were more German forces facing the British and Canadians than confronted the Americans. But this was an inescapable concomitant of the terrain. The Caen-Falaise plain leading directly to Paris was the most threatening approach to the Germans, and this they sought to block. Furthermore, because this was the only portion of the front where

The smoldering ruins of Caen after the entry of the British

the ground could sustain tank operations, the Germans placed their armored forces there.

Conversely, Montgomery's British and Canadian forces were stronger than those on the American side of the front, and for the same reasons. Armor could operate in the Caen-Falaise area, and there, along the shortest road to Paris, Eisenhower expected the main effort to be made.

Towards the end of June, as American troops were capturing Cherbourg, Montgomery informed Eisenhower that he was launching a 'blitz attack' in the Caen area. 'Once it starts,' he said, 'I will continue battle on the eastern flank till one of us cracks and it will not be us.'

Heartened by this indication of a concentrated British and Canadian push, Eisenhower was disappointed a few days later when Montgomery called off the attack. In Eisenhower's opinion, Montgomery had been slow

and cautious in pushing his advance.

With Cherbourg in Allied hands and undergoing extensive rehabilitation, Bradley's American forces turned south in the Cotentin. Since Montgomery was making little progress on the left part of the front, Bradley's troops would now have to launch a major attack in the hedgerow country.

Montgomery rationalized this reversed concept by saying that while he pinned down the bulk of the German defenders on the left, the Americans would make the breakout on the right. Yet if Montgomery had anticipated this development in the campaign – as he later claimed – it was a discredit to his foresight that he ordered no proper preparations to enable the Americans to get through the hedgerow country more quickly.

Bradley's First Army during the first two weeks of its offensive operations in July gained less than ten miles at a tremendous cost in casualties. As Eisenhower explained to Marshall, 'The going is extremely tough' because of the fighting quality

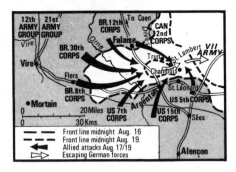

Battle of the pocket

of the German soldiers and the nature of the countryside. Furthermore, it rained almost incessantly during most of July, and the bad weather compelled a serious curtailment of close support air operations.

After meeting with Tedder and Smith early in July, both of whom felt that Montgomery was too cautious, Eisenhower wrote Montgomery a tactful letter. 'It appears to me,' he said, 'that we must use all possible energy in a determined effort to prevent a stalemate or of facing the necessity of fighting a major defensive battle with the slight depth we now have in the bridgehead.'

He was referring to the fact that the beachhead on the left, where Caen still remained in enemy hands, was too slender to be considered secure.

Montgomery answered at once, saying that he was 'quite happy about the situation.' He was working, he said, on a 'very definite plan.' He was planning to 'set my eastern flank alight,' seize Caen and get bridgeheads across the Orne river, which flows through the town. The British army was going to put on a 'big show' and Montgomery was going to 'put everything into it.'

Eisenhower was, of course, delighted.

That evening, 460 bombers dropped 2,300 tons of high explosive on the approaches to Caen, and on the following morning, Canadian and British ground troops attacked. Three days later, Montgomery called off the offensive effort. He had taken half of Caen, that part on the near side of the Orne river, but he had stopped short of getting the bridgeheads across the river.

On that day, Bradley visited Montgomery and admitted that he was discouraged by the relative lack of progress on the American front. The hedgerows were simply too numerous and too well organized by the Germans to be taken quickly.

Montgomery told him to take all the time he needed. He would continue to attract the bulk of the enemy forces to his side of the front.

After Bradley departed, Dempsey, commander of the British Second Army, who had been present at the conversation between Montgomery and Bradley, suggested to the Allied ground force commander that perhaps the British might do more than simply pull Germans to their front. Given the difficulties of operating in the hedgerow country, the British and Canadians could perhaps engineer a breakthrough of the enemy positions.

Montgomery's first reaction was negative, but later that day he told Dempsey to build up a corps of three armored divisions for what he called a 'massive stroke' to be launched from Caen to Falaise. This attack would be codenamed GOODWOOD.

In apprising Eisenhower of his new plan, Montgomery again raised high hopes of an operation that would allow the Allies to break out of their constrained beachhead. 'My whole eastern flank will burst into flames.' he informed Eisenhower. GOODWOOD 'may have far-reaching results.' Two days later, he told Tedder, 'Plan if successful promises to be decisive.'

Once again Eisenhower was enthusiastic. He wrote to Montgomery about the 'brilliant stroke which will knock loose our present shackles. . . . I would not be at all surprised to see you gaining a victory that will make

Rapid deployment of British troops on discovery of a German strongpoint

some of the "old classics" look like a skirmish between patrols.'

Tedder assured Montgomery that 'All the air forces will be full out to support your far-reaching and decisive plan to the utmost of their ability.'

On 18th July, nearly 1,700 heavy bombers and almost 400 medium and light bombers dropped about 8,000 tons of bombs in the heaviest and most concentrated air attack in direct support of ground troops ever made. Following this bombardment, the ground troops moved forward. They were on the verge of achieving a clean penetration, but the Germans recovered, and the attack bogged down. Montgomery pushed the offensive for four days. He gained the rest of Caen and thirty-four square miles of ground. In the process he lost 500 tanks and more than 4,000 men.

Constrained to halt his attack because of his losses, Montgomery said he was satisfied that he had accomplished his purpose. He had worn down the Germans.

Those who had expected a decisive breakthrough were profoundly disappointed, especially Eisenhower.

Montgomery later tried to explain why 'a number of misunderstandings' had arisen over his objectives in GOODWOOD. He had been concerned only with 'a battle for position,' a preliminary operation to stimulate success on the part of the Americans.

Yet his earlier language, his promises of a decisive victory, seemed to contradict him. He had led his superior, Eisenhower, into believing that the British would break across the Orne river and speed to Falaise, which would make it much easier for the Americans to move through and out of the hedgerows. He had used up tanks and men in such amounts as to indicate a major effort. And he had moved only a few miles down the road from Caen to Falaise.

Although Montgomery could be

faulted on several grounds, his gravest fault was to have misled Eisenhower. If indeed he was trying for no breakthrough, as he later claimed, why had he led Eisenhower into anticipating such decisive results?

Keeping his patience in check, Eisenhower wrote to Montgomery on 21st July to ask whether they saw 'eye to eye on the big problems'. The Allies, he said, had certain objectives. They needed more space in Normandy for maneuver, for the location of supply installations and additional troops, for the building of airfields; they needed to destroy the German military forces; they needed to get to Brittany and overrun the ancient province for the ports there.

Eisenhower said he had been 'extremely hopeful and optimistic' that GOODWOOD 'assisted by tremendous air attack' would have a decisive effect on the battle of Normandy. That did not come about.

He was therefore 'pinning our immediate hopes on Bradley's attack'.

He urged Montgomery to continue offensive operations on his part of the front. Eventually, he reminded Montgomery, the United States would have more strength on the continent than Britain, but 'while we have equality in size we must go forward shoulder to shoulder, with honors and sacrifices equally shared.'

Eisenhower was pinning his hopes on an operation Bradley had code-named COBRA. 'A breakthrough at this juncture will minimize the total cost,' Eisenhower informed Bradley; 'pursue every advantage with an ardor verging on recklessness.' If Bradley obtained a breakthrough at this point in the campaign, 'the results will be incalculable.'

Bradley's operation, like Montgomery's at Caen and for GOODWOOD,

Eisenhower autographs currency for his men. The previous day, July 25th, he learned that several hundred soldiers had been killed by Allied bombs which fell short

General Lesley A McNair was among the victims of the incident

used heavy bombers in direct support of ground troops. More than 1,500 heavies dropped 3,300 tons of bombs, almost 400 medium bombers unleashed another 650 tons, and 550 fighter-bombers let go 200 additional tons on a carpet just below the Periers-St Lô road. The effect produced a minor earthquake.

Eisenhower had gone to Normandy that morning of 25th July to witness the bombardment and the initial attack. He was excited by the armada of bombers that appeared, but he was depressed when he learned that some of the bombs had fallen short. They had killed several hundred soldiers, including General Lesley McNair, the Army Ground Forces commander who had come from the United States on an inspection trip. Furthermore, first reports of Bradley's ground attack indicated that not much had been accomplished by the bombing. The going on the ground was slow. .

As Eisenhower boarded his plane to return to England, he told Bradley he would never again use heavy bombers in direct support of tactical troops. 'That's a job for artillery,' he said. 'I gave them a green light this time. But I promise you it's the last.'

He would later change his mind. For the COBRA bombardment had opened a gaping hole in the German defenses, and this soon became apparent.

The COBRA attack picked up speed. By 27th July, with the situation clarified and the extent of the penetration clear, Bradley shifted into high gear. Changing his orders in the midst of his attack, he propelled COBRA from a relatively limited offensive concerned with capturing Coutances into a breakthrough targeted on Avranches. Coutances fell on 28th July and, three days later, American troops had rolled thirty miles forward to gain Avranches at the base of the Cotentin peninsula, the symbolic entrance into Brittany.

The swift movement of the forces on the right of the Allied line dissolved the incipient threat of static warfare and sent the Allies into a war of movement.

Despite Montgomery's discouraging slowness and caution, despite the inhibiting effect of the hedgerows on Bradley, Eisenhower had dispersed the threat of static warfare, the possibility of a stalemate, the horror of a war of attrition.

Brittany, sticking westward into the Atlantic Ocean, had always been a significant objective of the pre-invasion planning, particularly because the port of Brest, on the tip of the peninsula, was closer to the United States than any other harbor on the continent. In the First World War, Brest had served as the port of entry for the bulk of American men, equipment, and supplies funneled to France; and the planners in the Second World War saw it as able to perform the same function once again. To make it useful, the Allies would have to conquer Brittany, take Brest, and preserve the railroad that tied the port to the interior of France.

As Brittany came within reach at the end of July, the command structure changed. The First Canadian Army became operational under Sir Henry D G Crerar. This gave Montgomery's 21st Army Group control of two armies, Dempsey's British Second

General H D G Crerar, commanding First Canadian Army

Avranches, the entrance to Brittany, falls to Bradley

and Crerar's Canadian First.

At the same time, Patton's US Third Army became operational. As Courtney Hodges took command of the US First Army, Bradley stepped up to command the 12th Army Group. With Bradley and Montgomery each controlling and directing two armies on a co-equal basis, it would have been logical for Eisenhower to take direct command of the two army groups. But because it had been impossible to bring SHAEF to the continent and establish in Normandy the extensive facilities the headquarters required – for example, communications – Montgomery continued to function as the Allied ground commander.

The strategy then being followed by the four Allied armies was to have three armies wheel eastward, lining up to face the Seine and the bulk of the German forces in Normandy, while the fourth under Patton moved westward into Brittany in force. The function of Patton's army, turning

westward from Avranches toward Brest, was to capture the railroad and the port, to seize several minor ports on the north shore of Brittany – St Malo, Cancale, St Brieuc, and Morlaix – and to bottle up sizable contingents of Germans who were holding the ports of Lorient and St Nazaire on the southern shore, ports that would be unnecessary for the Allies if they quickly captured Brest.

The complete disintegration of the German defenses in the American portion of the front soon led Eisenhower to change the course of this pre-invasion strategy. On 2nd August, he decided to turn the main weight of the Allied offensive eastward. The capture of Britanny and Brest became a minor effort. The prime objective became the destruction of the German forces in Normandy west of the Seine river. To this end, Patton sent only one corps westward; he developed his major thrust to the east on the right flank of the three other Allied armies.

This was a far-reaching change and on 4th August Montgomery issued a

US troops warily thread the narrow streets of St Malo

The battle in the countryside continues to be tough

new directive to govern the movement. Now, as the wheeling action turned, the Allied armies were to sweep the Germans out of the lodgment area and back across the Seine, destroying them in the process.

As this maneuver was picking up momentum, the Germans launched a surprising action. On the night of 7th August they turned and sprang. Sending several panzer divisions through Mortain to recapture Avranches, the Germans overran Mortain and placed the Allied wheeling movement in jeopardy. The Germans called it the Avranches counterattack. The Allies called it the Mortain counterattack.

Eisenhower was in Normandy on 8th August, the day after the Germans struck. Visiting Bradley's headquarters, he considered with his subordinate the two alternatives that were open. Bradley could stop the wheeling operation in order to destroy the German counterattack. Or he could continue the operation while containing the German blow.

107

German forces suffer heavily in the Argentan-Falaise pocket; most escape, nevertheless, before the pocket is closed

Bradley inclined toward the latter course of action, and Eisenhower agreed with him. If the Germans pushed westward while the Allies moved ever eastward on the wings, as Eisenhower informed Marshall, 'we have a good chance to encircle and destroy a lot of his [the enemy's] forces.'

The chance was particularly good because the Canadians had attacked from Caen toward Falaise on 7th August. If they pushed well toward Falaise, they would threaten the northern flank of the German counter-attacking forces.

While American troops under Hodges were standing and fighting in the Mortain area and others under Patton were driving ahead on the right flank, Bradley telephoned Montgomery. It was 8th August. He suggested that Patton turn the axis of his advance from the east to the

north. By swinging northward, he would head toward the British and Canadians coming down from Caen toward Falaise. If the British-Canadians and Americans met, say, at Argentan, they would trap the Germans in an immense pocket.

Montgomery thought that would be splendid. 'Obviously,' he said later in a formal directive, 'if we can close the gap completely, we shall have put the enemy in the most awkward predicament.'

Patton's troops reached the outskirts of Argenten on 13th August. There they were at the inter-army group boundary. This was a line drawn by Montgomery to keep the British Canadians and the Americans from interfering one with the other. Although Patton's men could have continued northward beyond Argentan, for there were few Germans opposing them, they would be forced to enter territory reserved to the British-Canadians. Bradley therefore ordered them to halt. He had no wish to have a collision with the Canadians coming down toward Falaise.

This left a twenty-five mile opening between the Americans and Canadians, and through this gap the Germans began to escape. As the Germans started to pull back from Mortain and move out of the pocket through the gap, Montgomery ordered the Canadians and Americans to close the opening by a meeting at Trun. They did so on the evening of 19th August. By then, the bulk of the Germans

Argentan still burns

had extricated themselves from the pocket.

Although the Germans lost about 10,000 dead and another 50,000 taken prisoner, they managed to get most of their troops and, with one or two exceptions, their headquarters, out of the Argentan-Falaise pocket.

Why were the Germans permitted

to escape? The criticism fell for the most part on Montgomery who had failed to move the inter-army group boundary to let the pocket be closed from the south by the Americans. Yet Bradley was at fault too, for he had avoided mentioning the subject to Montgomery. He felt that setting boundaries between the army groups was completely Montgomery's prerogative.

If both commanders were practising the good manners of coalition warfare, Eisenhower might have stepped in to order the pocket closed earlier. Instead, he preferred to let his field commanders make the decisions.

'Due to the extraordinary defensive measures taken by the enemy,' Eisenhower informed Marshall, 'it is possible that our total bag of prisoners [in the Argentan-Falaise pocket] will not be so great as I first anticipated.'

This was, of course, only half the story. The other half was that Eisenhower had refrained from interfering in the details of the battle of the pocket in order to preserve the closeness of the coalition command structure. In doing so, he sacrificed what might have been an even more decisive victory. For the enemy troops who escaped from the pocket lived to fight another day.

This was rather obscure at the end of August, when the spectre of static warfare seemed to have vanished for good, when the liberation of Paris was at hand, when the war seemed about to end. It was then that Eisenhower decided to cross the Seine at once instead of waiting to build up his logistical installations as the preinvasion plans had projected.

At this point, as the Normandy campaign was coming to a close, Eisenhower had to deal with another controversy, a disagreement that stemmed from the divergence in thought and opinion between him and his chief lieutenant, Montgomery.

Broad Front

The commander meets men of the 29th
Infantry Division

The explosion generated by Operation COBRA turned into a whirlwind that swept the Germans across the Seine with the Allied armies in hot pursuit.

In the pre-invasion planning, OVER-LORD was projected only as far as the Seine. The planners expected the Germans to defend at the Seine and the Allies to pause there. Only after regrouping their forces and building up their logistical structure would the Allies try to cross.

Yet as early as 7th August Eisenhower told Marshall that he was thinking 'to cross the Seine before the enemy has time to hold it in strength.' Ten days later he decided to 'dash across the Seine' without stopping. And on 19th August he ordered crossings in strength. The next objective

was the German border, more than 250 miles away.

Beyond that was the Rhine. Across the river, the Allied forces would head for the Ruhr, encircle that great German industrial complex, and destroy Germany's capacity to wage war.

What made this thrilling outlook feasible was Eisenhower's hope that the British-Canadians, after crossing the lower Seine, would secure the Channel ports – Le Havre, Dieppe, Boulogne, Calais, Dunkerque, Ostend, and, most important of all, Antwerp. With sufficient ports of entry near the fighting front, Eisenhower believed he could sustain the momentum of what was turning into a gigantic pursuit.

When Eisenhower ordered the Allied armies across the Seine, he announced that he would take personal command of the ground forces on 1st September. This was in consonance with pre-invasion plans. Montgomery was, as the military say, wearing two hats. In addition to acting as the temporary commander of the ground forces, he was 21st Army Group commander. It had long been decided that upon the completion of OVERLORD – that is, when the lodgment area was seized – Eisenhower would replace Montgomery as ground forces commander. Montgomery would revert to his position at the head of his 21st Army Group. Eisenhower would then wear two hats; he would be the Supreme Allied Commander and the ground forces commander. In the latter capacity he would control directly the operations of Montgomery's 21st Army Group and Bradley's 12th Army Group.

There is little doubt that if Montgomery had performed more loyally in Normandy, he would have remained ground forces commander for the remainder of the campaign.

Having announced his decision to change the command structure, Eisenhower indicated the paths to be taken by his army groups. Montgomery was to advance north of the

Above: The Seine is bridged and the first troops cross. *Below:* Bombs blanket V1 launch sites in Northern France. These installations are recognized by Eisenhower to be among the prime objectives in Montgomery's projected overrunning of the Pas de Calais

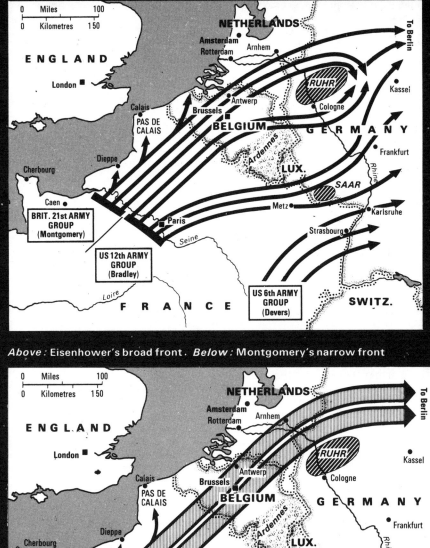

Above: Eisenhower's broad front. *Below:* Montgomery's narrow front

Ardennes, that is, north-east to Antwerp, then on to the Ruhr. Bradley was to go south of the Ardennes, that is, eastward to Metz, then on to the Saar, a lesser though still important German industrial area, and finally move to the Ruhr. Once there, both army groups would encircle the major industrial complex of Germany.

Although these events seemed near at hand in the exhilarating days of the pursuit, they belonged to the distant future.

Reacting on 23rd August to Eisenhower's general scheme of advance, Montgomery suggested that sending the 21st and 12th Army Groups around the northern and southern edges of the Ardennes, thereby separating them, would be a mistake. He proposed instead to have them remain together in one compact force. If they both moved around the northern edge of the Ardennes in a 'solid mass', as Montgomery put it, of some forty divisions, they would be so strong that they 'need fear nothing'. This steamroller, he envisioned, could move irresistibly to the German border, to the Rhine and across it, and, bypassing the Ruhr, strike directly for Berlin. The Germans were about to collapse, Montgomery believed, and he thought that a single thrust under a single commander, meaning Montgomery himself, was the quickest way to end the war.

Eisenhower rejected the single thrust proposal. There is no question but that he misunderstood Montgomery's idea, for he referred to the scheme as a 'knifelike' thrust.

Yet he had sound reasons for the alternative he had in mind, an advance all along the front. He believed that moving in only one area was to invite the Germans to rip into the flanks of that force. He wanted, as he later said, to have 'more than one string to our bow'. What he wished to do was to progress on a broad front and thereby stretch the German defenses. This would make it impossible for them to stop the Allied movement anywhere.

He also felt that an all-out, headlong drive to Berlin was completely impractical. There were other objectives that needed to be taken first. He wanted a more methodical approach, and in a sense he was acting cautiously. Montgomery had suddenly become reckless.

At the same time, Eisenhower recognised that Montgomery was heading into a region where the most important immediate and intermediate Allied objectives lay. By overrunning the Pas de Calais, Montgomery would eliminate the last sizable German force in western Europe, destroy the V-weapon launching sites from which the buzz bombs started on their flights which were striking England cruelly, gain vital airfields, and seize the great port of Antwerp.

Antwerp was particularly on Eisenhower's mind. It would be close to the developing Allied front, much more convenient than Cherbourg, already far to the rear, than Marseilles, which was about to be taken but would still be distant, and Brest, which remained for the moment – until the end of September – in German hands.

The reason for Eisenhower's interest in Antwerp was that he was becoming concerned about the shaky logistical system. The units taking part in the pursuit across the Seine would soon outrun their supplies. 'Right now,' he wrote Marshall on 24th August, 'we are operating on the basis of having today's supplies only with each division and are accumulating no fat,' meaning no reserves in fuel, ammunition, and other items needed to sustain the advance. 'The decision as to exactly what to do at this moment has taken a lot of anxious thought because . . . we do not have sufficient strength and supply possibilities to do everything we should like to do simultaneously.'

What was happening was that the surge of troops across Normandy and into northern France had prevented an orderly and systematic development of the logistical organization. Instead of setting up depots for the storage of supplies close to the combat units, the Allied forces were hurriedly bringing supplies directly from the original invasion beaches and from Cherbourg up forward for immediate use by the combat troops. As the distance between the Normandy coast and the front lengthened, so did round trips. Trucks were wearing out because they were in constant use. Railroads had been destroyed by air attacks. The flow of supplies dwindled to a trickle.

Antwerp was thus significant for the execution of future plans. And Eisenhower consequently acceded partially to Montgomery's proposal. He told Bradley to send one of his two armies, the First, north of the Ardennes to strengthen Montgomery in what would be the main Allied effort. Yet Eisenhower insisted on maintaining the momentum of Bradley's thrust south of the Ardennes and toward the Saar, now definitely a subsidiary operation, in order to fashion a southern prong for the eventual encirclement of the Ruhr.

Meanwhile, an Allied force on 15th August had landed in southern France. This was the disputed ANVIL operation that Eisenhower had persisted in calling for over the protests of Churchill and other British strategists. After taking the port of Marseilles, Allied troops rushed up the Rhône valley and joined Eisenhower's OVERLORD forces on 15th September. At that time Devers, commander of the 6th Army Group and directing a French Army and an American Army, came under Eisenhower's command.

This gave Eisenhower three army group commanders, Montgomery, Bradley, and Devers, and control over land forces that covered a front from Holland to the Mediterranean, from the Atlantic almost to the German border. On 20th September, Eisenhower opened his headquarters at Versailles; he established an advance command post at Reims.

By then, the debate over whether to pursue a broad-front strategy or a narrow-front movement had reached a head. Early in September, with the Germans apparently on the verge of collapse and the war seemingly drawing to a close, Eisenhower's broad-front advance became a stampede. Its object was to keep the Germans, Eisenhower said, 'stretched everywhere.'

On 4th September, Montgomery resumed his attempt to change the nature of the pursuit. 'I consider,' he wrote to Eisenhower, 'we have now reached a stage where one really powerful and full-blooded thrust towards Berlin is likely to get there and thus end the German war.'

Since the Allies lacked the resources to sustain two full-blooded offensives, one by the 21st Army Group, the other by the 12th Army Group – the 6th Army Group was still to join – Montgomery suggested concentrating the available strength in a single thrust. The Ruhr was, obviously, a more important target than the Saar. 'If we attempt a compromise solution and split our maintenance [logistical] resources so that neither thrust [meaning his and Bradley's] is full-blooded,' he warned, 'we will prolong the war.'

Eisenhower replied on the following day. A broad advance, he reiterated, would give the Allies freedom to strike anywhere while forcing the enemy to be thin everywhere. His chief aim remained flexibility, the ability to meet whatever resistance the Germans could manage to offer and wherever it appeared. Yet he recognised, he repeated, that Montgomery was moving towards the more important targets and, to enable him to advance toward Antwerp, Eisenhower gave him priority to receive the major part of the dwindling supplies of Allied fuel and ammunition.

Unsaid in Eisenhower's position was the fact that he could not sanction a single thrust executed either by

In the south of France troops of operation ANVIL advance through pine woods in the dawn

Americans or British because both, rather than one or ther other, had to win the war. He was unable to allow a single advance under the command of Montgomery, who had a justifiable reputation for caution. He was similarly unable to place Montgomery under Bradley or Patton, for Montgomery was the senior officer of Eisenhower's subordinates. Further, if he stopped Bradley's American advance and gave all the supplies to Montgomery, the American public would be outraged. And if he stopped Montgomery and backed Bradley with all his might, the British public would raise an outcry.

Thus, although Eisenhower was motivated primarily by his military outlook, that is, his desire to advance on a broad front to keep the Germans stretched, he was aware of underlying political or public relations factors that bolstered his thinking.

Montgomery protested again on 7th September, and asked Eisenhower to come and meet him for a discussion of the issue.

Eisenhower went to see him on the 10th. By this time, the Germans were settling into the West Wall – the Siegfried Line, as the Allies called it. In these long-abandoned fortifications along the German border, the Germans determined to stand and fight.

There the Allied forces ran out of the fuel, ammunition, and rations in the amounts they needed to crack the West Wall defenses. This was clearer in retrospect than it was at the time. Nevertheless, there were indications that the pursuit was about to come to an end at the German frontier.

During his conference with Eisenhower, Montgomery repeated his belief that the Allied armies lacked the power for all of them to get to the Rhine. Only if Eisenhower halted some forces and diverted their fuel and

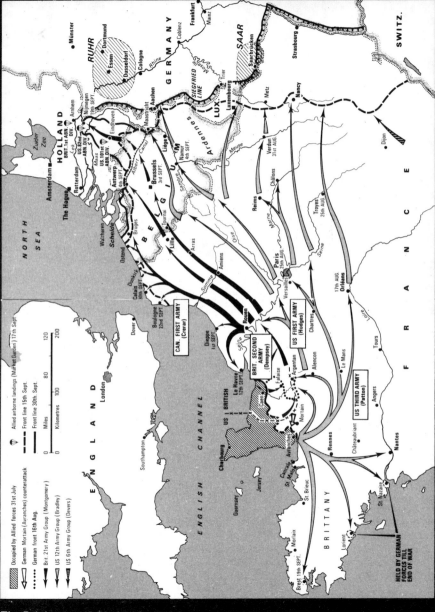

The Falaise gap and broad front offensive to the German border

German forces quickly deploy to meet the threat of the Arnhem-Nijmegen operation, MARKET-GARDEN

ammunition to the others could he hope to propel the Allies across the Rhine to the Ruhr. Obviously, since Montgomery's advance was the major Allied effort, it was he who should get virtually all the Allied supplies.

As the first step of this grand concept, Montgomery proposed an operation named MARKET-GARDEN. Daring, if not downright risky, it was a plan to use airborne and armored divisions to get across the lower Rhine in the Netherlands.

Montgomery wished to use the three divisions of the First Allied Airborne Army to spread a carpet of troops along a narrow corridor into the Netherlands and jump the lower Rhine. These troops were to be stitched together by an armored thrust up that corridor. If he could get across the river barrier, he would outflank the West Wall positions and be ready, assuming he could get the necessary supplies, for a drive directly towards

the Ruhr.

Part of his own narrow-front outlook, Montgomery saw this operation as an alternative to Eisenhower's broad-front strategy.

To accept Montgomery's idea meant deferring the employment of the port of Antwerp. The city had been captured early in September, but before the port could be used, the more than fifty-mile stretch of the Schelde estuary had to be cleared. In their retreat from Normandy, German forces had taken firm control of the shores of this inlet and had mined the water approaches to the harbor. If Montgomery gave his major attention to MARKET-GARDEN, he would be unable to give first priority to Antwerp.

Eisenhower accepted Montgomery's recommendation, not merely because he approved abandoning the broad-front concept. Rather, he was willing to make use of the airborne forces,

Allied corpses litter the streets of Arnhem in the latter stages of the operation

which, since the invasion and the early days of June, had been idle in Britain and awaiting an opportunity to get into action again.

As Eisenhower explained to Marshall, he was always willing to 'defer capture of ports in favor of bolder and more rapid movement to the front.' But with winter coming, he needed Antwerp. He told Marshall that 'it is absolutely imperative' for Montgomery to take Antwerp after MARKET-GARDEN.

MARKET-GARDEN started on 17th September. A week later it was over. Although Montgomery carved an Allied corridor sixty-five miles deep into the Netherlands and secured bridgeheads over the Maas and Waal Rivers, he failed to jump the Rhine or to outflank the West Wall. He had lost almost 12,000 men but had failed to push a supposedly tottering German government into collapse.

With that, the Allied pursuit, which had sputtered out around the middle of September, came to a definite halt.

Once again, despite the evidence that MARKET-GARDEN furnished any single thrust had small chance of succeeding against a Germany that was not yet finished, that would indeed fight on for another seven months – Montgomery asked that everything be put into his own 21st Army Group advance for an immediate drive towards Berlin.

Eisenhower refused.

On 22nd September he told Montgomery categorically to devote all his energies to clearing the Germans from the Schelde so that the port of Antwerp could be opened.

Preoccupied with getting across the Rhine in the Netherlands, Montgomery had overlooked the importance of the Schelde, which could earlier have been cleared almost for the asking. It would take the Canadian army more than two months to clear the estuary. On 28th November, with the shores taken from the Germans and the waters swept of mines, the first Allied ship entered the port.

By then, the campaign in western Europe had entered the phase of hard and bitter fighting. The high expectations of a quick end to the war had vanished. The Germans were strongly entrenched along the West Wall. No real offensive could be mounted until spring.

After the war, Montgomery charged

US troops march through Nijmegen

that 'we advanced to the Rhine on several fronts, which were unco-ordinated.' It was his contention still that a single thrust might have won the war. Yet the evidence points to the contrary conclusion. The absence of a firm logistical structure to sustain an Allied drive, together with the resuscitation of the German defense at the West Wall, plus the inability of the Allies to use Antwerp, meant that the war had not yet run its course. The failure of MARKET-GARDEN underscored that reality.

The Bulge

Eisenhower strides past a wrecked
German tank

The Allied campaign in western Europe during the fall and winter of 1944 registered daily gains in yards rather than in miles. The Germans had recovered from their defeat in Normandy and from their withdrawal across northern France. They held firmly, fighting desperately to give Hitler time to prepare a last counterblow. Bad weather helped them. So did continuing Allied supply shortages. The enemy's 'continued solid resistance,' Eisenhower noted on 20th November, 'is a main factor postponing final victory.'

Montgomery still was trying to promote a single thrust strategy, not only because he believed in this method of winning but also because he wished to have command of the Allied ground

forces again.

Churchill and Brooke supported Montgomery but not to the point where they were willing to make an issue of the strategy that would result in the relief of one commander or the other.

Eisenhower resisted the pressure. His only concession was that when good weather came in the spring of 1945, he would launch the major Allied stroke in the north under Montgomery. But he would keep Bradley and Devers moving into Germany in subsidiary operations.

As the campaign dragged on, with little drama to alleviate the bitter struggle, a sudden eruption on 16th December blossomed into the gravest threat to Allied success. This was Hitler's Ardennes counteroffensive.

It opened at dawn, when twenty four German divisions struck three American divisions holding a seventy-five-mile front in the Ardennes. The Germans smashed through this thin line, achieved complete surprise, and crushed two divisions.

No one had expected an offensive of this proportion. The Allies had not suspected that the Germans had been capable of collecting such large reserves. They were taken aback also by the location of the German attack. Rolling forested countryside penetrated by few good roads, it was hardly an area through which to commit the mechanized forces of *blitzkrieg*. But the Allied intelligence officers had forgotten that the Germans had broken through the Ardennes in 1940, as they had in 1870.

Eisenhower, as usual, accepted the blame. Lacking a real strategic reserve, for the great bulk of his forces was engaged in offensive operations, he decided to take the two divisions that he had in reserve and commit them at the key point of Bastogne. He counted on an armored division. already fighting to hold at the other key point of St Vith. He also decided to send Patton north to Bastogne to stick the flank of the German forces

Above : German POWs dig graves for men of 101st Airborne Division who died defending Bastogne
Below : Völksgrenadier infantrymen captured in the Ardennes counteroffensive

pushing an increasingly larger bulge into the American lines.

Hitler hoped to reach Antwerp, which was his strategic objective. The Allies believed that he was trying only to get across the Meuse River to split the 12th and 21st Army Groups and give the Germans a tactical advantage. Yet even this threat was serious. Once the Allies were divided, the Germans had a good chance of racing through Allied rear areas and creating havoc and confusion.

Unable to do more immediately than to form the shape of his counterefforts, Eisenhower tried to get more infantry replacements for the divisions holding the front. He circularized Communications Zone installations, those engaged in supply operations, asking for men who were willing to be trained as infantrymen. He also invited Negroes who were serving in segregated units to volunteer for integrated combat duty.

In those days black soldiers were mainly regarded as being fit for duty only as truck drivers and stevedores. There were a few exceptions – a Negro infantry division was fighting in Italy and several armored and artillery units were fighting in western Europe. But Eisenhower's call for black soldiers to enter white units on a basis of equality was an unorthodox measure.

Bedell Smith, Eisenhower's chief of staff, was outraged. Citing the regulations that laid down the separation of the races in army units, Smith remonstrated that the American public would take offense if Eisenhower carried through his intent to integrate combat units. Furthermore, so drastic a step would indicate a reaction to the Ardennes counteroffensive that could be construed as bordering on panic.

Eisenhower retracted his original invitation. Thousands of Negroes, nevertheless, volunteered to become infantrymen and enter combat. They were trained quickly, then formed into segregated platoons and inserted into white rifle companies. It was a cruel disappointment for men who had

Bedell Smith raised strong objections to Eisenhower's proposal to integrate black and white American units

hoped to break the repressive color line that relegated them to second-class citizenship.

By the time they were trained to enter combat, the danger of the Bulge had passed. Fighting as parts of regular infantry companies, platoons of colored soldiers throughout the American forces in western Europe performed in magnificent fashion during the final months of the war in 1945.

The German attack through the Ardennes produced discouragement in the Allied camp. Not only was it completely unexpected, but no one dreamed that the Germans could make an effort of this magnitude so close to what seemed like the end of the war. A feeling of malaise, of psychological disturbance, affected the Allied forces. Victory had seemed quite near, and suddenly the Germans had risen again.

Contributing to widespread feelings of anxiety was the knowledge that special groups of German soldiers had infiltrated into the Allied lines. Hitler had authorized the formation of units composed of English-

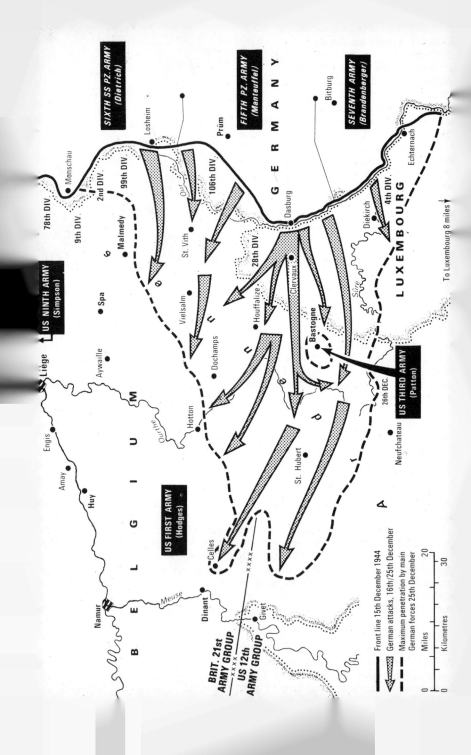

speaking Germans dressed in American uniforms. Their purpose was to spearhead the advance elements in the attack and spread confusion. This they did along the battleline.

Rumors soon started that these Germans in American dress were out to assassinate Eisenhower. A vast security effort in the American camp was immediately implemented. Military policemen stopped vehicles everywhere and asked special questions that would identify Americans – who was Mickey Mouse's wife? Betty Grable's husband? who had won the World Series in baseball that year? Only Americans were likely to know the answers.

At the same time, Eisenhower lost most of his freedom of movement. A huge guard accompanied him wherever he went.

Three days after the initial attack, by 19th December, the development of the Germans thrust began to cut Bradley's forces in two. Communications from Bradley's headquarters to some of his subordinate units became a problem. If Bradley was about to lose touch with and be unable to direct certain units in the battle, it made sense to place those elements under Montgomery. If Eisenhower decided to do so, Bradley would have to relinquish command of the US First and Ninth Armies and keep control only of the Third.

Reluctant to put this shift in command into effect, Eisenhower made the decision on 20th December.

On the same day, he learned that he had been promoted to five-star rank, General of the Army, one of four Army officers to be so honored – together with Marshall, MacArthur, and Arnold. It was a vote of confidence in Eisenhower's abilities, and it came at a critical moment. The Battle of the Bulge would have to be resolved satisfactorily if that high distinction in grade was to mean anything.

In the next few days, the Germans seemed to be winning. There was some grumbling among Americans over the

December 1944. Eisenhower's car displays the insignia of his new rank : General of the Army

command shift, which seemed almost to have reinstated Montgomery as ground forces commander. Bad weather was preventing Allied aircraft from flying, a condition the Germans had anticipated, and the ground troops lacked support from the air. Bastogne was still holding out although encircled. The defenders of St Vith were in a precarious position.

At this discouraging time, Eisenhower received a letter from Marshall that gave him renewed vigor. Marshall had written to say that Eisenhower's leadership, wisdom, patience, and tolerance had 'made possible Allied cooperation and teamwork in the greatest military operation in the history of the world, complicated by social, economic and political problems almost without precedent. You have my complete confidence.'

St Vith fell on 23rd December, but the armored division defending it managed to make an orderly withdrawal. These armored troops had gained time for Bradley and Montgomery to organize and stiffen the defenses. Bastogne still held.

The weather was clear on that day. Planes were able to fly for the first time in a week. Air drops to the defenders of Bastogne and air attacks on the German columns gave hope that the attack would soon be contained and turned back.

Three days later, elements of Patton's army reached Bastogne, broke through the ring encircling the town, and ended the threat that the Germans might smash forward to the Meuse.

As the situation for the Allies brightened, Montgomery suggested that the front be shortened to get better positions for an Allied counterattack. This meant withdrawing, giving up ground. Opposed to giving up ground, which would only encourage the Germans, Eisenhower saw little reason to extend the Bulge. Yet he realized and accepted the proposition that a flexible defense was better than rigidly holding all terrain.

On 26th December, as the Allied reaction to the German blow was developing favorably, Eisenhower indicated to his subordinates that he wanted them to move over to the offensive and end the German threat. He instructed Devers to shift his positions and make ready to attack. He overruled Bradley who wanted the US First and Ninth Armies returned to his command. He approved Montgomery's desire to give up some ground if absolutely necessary, but he told him to hold the general line of defense. He restrained Bradley and Patton who were raring to go, and held them in check, the better to prepare for a 'methodical and sure' Allied counterattack. He also prodded Montgomery into formulating plans for sweeping the Germans out of the Bulge.

Montgomery responded on 27th December with a blueprint for an Allied attack. But he said he would be unable to go over to the offensive until sometime in January.

To Eisenhower this seemed to be too late. He remembered how the caution of his subordinates at Kasserine Pass had enabled Rommel to escape. Determined to avoid a repetition of this event, he traveled to meet with Montgomery in order to get him to move more quickly.

Montgomery hesitated to attack at once, for he expected the Germans to shift the axis of their attack northward, that is, against the main forces of his 21st Army Group.

Eisenhower talked him into agreeing to attack on 1st January.

His intention now was to destroy the Germans west of the Rhine. In many respects, this would be similar to the destruction of the German armies in Normandy west of the Seine. At Mortain the Germans had pushed their head into a noose fashioned at Argentan and Falaise and closed – but too late – at Trun. Once again, the Bulge constituted a potential noose. If it could be closed, the Allies would trap the Germans in the Ardennes.

In other words, since the German tide had been stemmed, if the Allies could attack before the tide flowed back, they would eliminate the bulk of the German military forces in western Europe. They would then face little opposition on their way to the Rhine and across. The war would be as good as won.

This, of course, depended on attacking the Germans before they extricated their forces from the Bulge.

On 30th December, Eisenhower received word that Montgomery would be unable to attack before 3rd January.

When Bradley, in conformity with the overall plan coordinated by Eisenhower, launched his offensive effort on 1st January, he soon discovered that the Germans had switched panzer divisions from the north, where Montgomery's forces were remaining quiet, to the south to stop Bradley.

On that day, Montgomery again asked for command of the Allied

ground forces.

That evening Eisenhower wrote a formal directive to govern future operations. He reiterated that Montgomery would make the major Allied thrust in the north, while Bradley engineered a secondary operation in the south. Montgomery was to retain control of the US Ninth Army, but he was to return the US First Army to Bradley. 'The one thing that must now be prevented.' Eisenhower specified. 'is the stabilization of the enemy salient [the Bulge] with infantry, permitting him opportunity to use his Panzers at will . . . We must regain the initiative, and speed and energy are essential.'

What he meant was that he would tolerate no delay on Montgomery's part in getting his attack under way.

He also sent a short personal note to Montgomery telling him there was no need for a single ground commander. The advance into Germany would be made on a broad front with Eisenhower himself coordinating the movement. Furthermore, he said, he would

Though here all seems amity, Eisenhower still had trouble getting Montgomery to act in concert with his other commanders

tolerate no more debate on the question of an overall ground command.

Montgomery attacked on 3rd January. It was somewhat late. No spectacular pocket was formed around the bulk of the German forces, and they fought their way out of the Bulge in skilful and orderly fashion.

On 7th February, the front that had been in existence at the time of the Ardennes counteroffensive was restored. By launching his dramatic offensive in an attempt to turn the course of the war, Hitler had expended most of his remaining armor and mobility. The military weakness resulting from that exertion indicated clearly that the Germans could have no hope of redressing the balance and securing victory.

Eisenhower had by then already outlined what would be the final campaign of the war.

Berlin

The Reichstag building burns for the
second time

On 20th January, Eisenhower indicated how he wished to eliminate Germany from the war. All his armies were to close on a broad front to the Rhine, seeking in the process to destroy the enemy. They were then to cross the Rhine and proceed to the heart of Germany.

The original instructions from the Combined Chiefs of Staff to Eisenhower had used the phrase in defining his mission but without specifying the location of the heart. They left it to Eisenhower to determine exactly what the heart of Germany was.

An obvious objective was Berlin, the capital. Reaching Berlin would signify for the Allies the end of the war. Yet Berlin was distant from the shores of western Europe, and from the begin-

ning of the European campaign in 1944 it was deemed too far to be a practical goal for the invading armies.

Much closer and within reach of the OVERLORD forces was the Ruhr. As Bedell Smith later said, the factories of the Ruhr 'pumped lifeblood into the [German] military system. Once the Ruhr was sealed off, the heart would cease to beat.'

The Ruhr area was a feasible objective for it was within range of the armies of the Western coalition. In contrast, Berlin was closer to the Eastern Front. The Red Army was approaching Berlin, and a simple glance at the map showed that the capital of Germany would very likely fall to the Russians. On 15th February, Russian forces reached the Oder-Niesse river line, thirty-five miles from Berlin, and secured bridgeheads across the water.

Had OVERLORD been launched in 1942 or 1943, Berlin might have made sense as a Western objective. The Russians had been driven far to the east into their territory and had yet to start their comeback.

In 1945, there was no question but that the Russians would get to Berlin. The Western Allies were more than 250 miles from the city.

Focusing his attention on the Ruhr, Eisenhower was supremely confident. The bugaboo of the Bulge had dissolved and the prospects looked promising. 'All our preparations are made,' Eisenhower informed Marshall, 'the troops are in fine fettle and there is no question in my mind that if we get off to a good start . . . the [final] operations will be a complete success.'

By early March the Allied forces were closing on the Rhine river. All the bridges were destroyed, either by Allied air attacks or by German demolition, all except one at Remagen. By a coup de main, the US First Army seized this structure intact, then started an immediate buildup of forces on the east bank. Later that month, Patton's Third Army jumped the Rhine on the run. Still later, after

The damaged Remagen bridge over the Rhine, key to Allied advance into Germany

meticulous preparations and a heavy preparatory artillery bombardment, Montgomery's 21st Army Group moved across. Devers' 6th Army Group also crossed the river.

With all the army groups across the Rhine, Eisenhower directed Montgomery and Bradley to surround the Ruhr. He sent Devers into southern Germany in subsidiary operations.

On 26th March, Montgomery informed Eisenhower that as soon as the Ruhr was encircled, he planned to move toward the Elbe. He meant Berlin.

To Eisenhower, Berlin had little significance. Like Rome, it had little importance as a military objective. Its value lay in its political and symbolic meaning. Although Eisenhower was well aware of Clausewitz's dictum that war is a continuation of politics by other means, he saw himself functioning as a military leader rather than as a political figure. As a military commander, his proper sphere of action was in determining military goals. His mission was to defeat the military forces of the enemy, which was also a precept out of Clausewitz. Setting political objectives was a responsibility that belonged to the political authorities, the President and the Prime Minister. Lacking specific instructions from them, Eisenhower formulated his plans on a military basis.

The military objective that remained was to destroy the enemy military machine, which, though on the verge of disintegration, still functioned, still defended the homeland, still inflicted losses on the Allied armies.

With this in mind, Eisenhower on 28th March made what would be his final change in the disposition of his army groups. In order to cut Germany in half and divide the German forces

Above : US and Russians meet on the Elbe. *Below :* Landing-craft are also used in the crossing of the Rhine once the bridgehead is secured

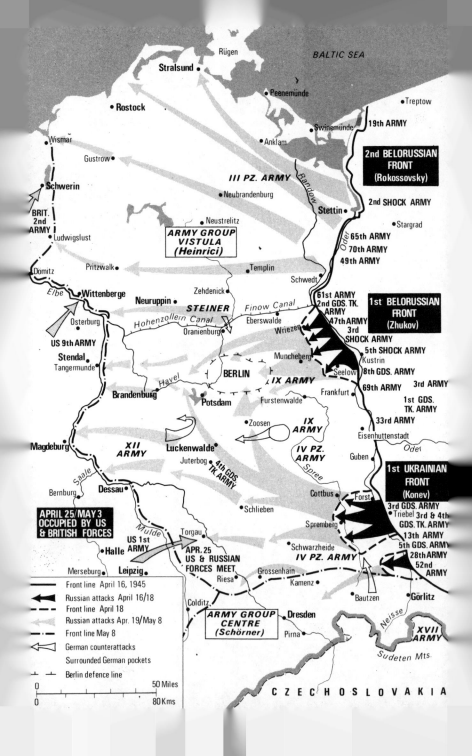

BALTIC SEA

Rügen

Stralsund

Peenemünde

Treptow

Rostock

Swinemünde

19th ARMY

Wismar

Anklam

2nd BELORUSSIAN FRONT (Rokossovsky)

Schwerin

Gustrow

III PZ. ARMY

Randow

Stettin

2nd SHOCK ARMY

Neubrandenburg

Stargrad

BRIT. 2nd ARMY

Ludwigslust

Neustrelitz

ARMY GROUP VISTULA (Heinrici)

Oder

65th ARMY
70th ARMY
49th ARMY

Domitz

Pritzwalk

Templin

Schwedt

Elbe

Wittenberge

Neuruppin

Zehdenick

STEINER

Finow Canal

61st ARMY
2nd GDS. TK. ARMY

1st BELORUSSIAN FRONT (Zhukov)

Osterburg

Hohenzollern Canal

Eberswalde

47th ARMY

Wriezen

US 9th ARMY

Oranienburg

3rd SHOCK ARMY

Stendal

Muncheberg

5th SHOCK ARMY

Tangermunde

Havel

BERLIN

IX ARMY

Seelow

Kustrin

8th GDS. ARMY

Brandenburg

Potsdam

Furstenwalde

Frankfurt

69th ARMY

3rd ARMY

1st GDS. TK. ARMY

Zoosen

IX ARMY

33rd ARMY

Magdeburg

XII ARMY

Luckenwalde

IV PZ. ARMY

Eisenhuttenstadt

Oder

Guben

1st UKRAINIAN FRONT (Konev)

Bernburg

Saale

Dessau

Juterbog

4th GDS. TK ARMY

Cottbus

Forst

3rd GDS. ARMY

APRIL 25/MAY 3 OCCUPIED BY US & BRITISH FORCES

Schlieben

Spremberg

Triebel

3rd & 4th GDS. TK. ARMY

13th ARMY

Mulde

Torgau

Schwarzheide

5th GDS. ARMY

28th ARMY

US 1st ARMY

APR. 25 US & RUSSIAN FORCES MEET

IV PZ. ARMY

52nd ARMY

Halle

Merseburg

Leipzig

Riesa

Grossenhain

Kamenz

Bautzen

Görlitz

Colditz

Front line April 16, 1945

Russian attacks April 16/18

Front line April 18

Russian attacks Apr. 19/May 8

Front line May 8

German counterattacks

Surrounded German pockets

Berlin defence line

ARMY GROUP CENTRE (Schörner)

Dresden

Pirna

Neisse

XVII ARMY

Sudeten Mts.

0   50 Miles
0   80 Kms

C Z E C H O S L O V A K I A

into pockets unable to offer serious resistance, Eisenhower shifted his main thrust from Montgomery in the north to Bradley in the center. He took the US Ninth Army from the operational control of Montgomery's 21st Army Group and placed it again under Bradley's 12th Army Group. With the preponderance of forces in western Europe directly under him, Bradley was to slash across the center of Germany to a meeting with the Russians near Dresden. Montgomery and Devers were to make secondary efforts in the north and south.

The British Chiefs of Staff objected. They informed Marshall that a proper course of action would be to continue the major effort in the north in order to open the German ports, nullify the U-boat menace, and liberate the southern approaches to Denmark.

Although the British said nothing specifically about Berlin, they were actually thinking of that objective. Whoever took Berlin, they believed, would receive the credit for having won the war.

Berlin occupied : Russian armor pours into the stricken city

Yet Berlin was in the occupation zone reserved to the Russians. The Allies had reached political agreement on the postwar occupation of Germany, and the Russian zone extended westward to the Elbe and Mulde Rivers, with Berlin well inside.

What the British Chiefs of Staff, speaking for Churchill, were saying was that if American and British troops moved on to territory reserved for the Russian occupation, they would act as a pressure force to compel the Russians to live up to the agreements they had made with the British and Americans on the postwar world. More specifically, if Western troops were lodged in the Russian zone of occupation at the end of the war, their withdrawal could be keyed to force the Russians to give the Western Allies access to Berlin. In terms of the future postwar conditions, Berlin was distinctly a political objective.

Replying to the British on 31st March, Eisenhower said: 'My plan is simple and aims at dividing and destroying the German forces and joining hands with the Red Army . . . [Berlin] has become . . . nothing but a geographical location, and I have never been interested in these. My purpose is to destroy the enemy's forces and his powers to resist.'

The Russians were still at the Oder-Neisse river line. For more than a month there had been little activity on that front. But it was obvious that the Russians could move the thirty-five miles into Berlin any time they wished. In contrast, the Western Allies were still more than 200 miles from the capital.

Since there was little likelihood of reaching Berlin before the Russians, Eisenhower was concerned by other considerations. There were rumors that the Germans were planning extensive guerrilla warfare. An underground army of 'Werewolves' youngsters trained for terrorist activities, was supposed to be in the process of formation to harass the Allies. In addition, there was talk of a German retreat in the Bavarian Alps, a natural defensive area, where Hitler and his government planned to make a last-ditch stand.

To dissolve these possibilities, which had nothing to do with Berlin, and to avoid a head-on collision with the Russians, which would have been a dangerous concomitant of a drive on Berlin, Eisenhower decided to conform to the prevailing military theory and destroy the enemy armed forces. Berlin would hardly serve this purpose.

Furthermore, since the zones of occupation were already drawn, Eisenhower saw no reason to push his troops beyond the border of the Russian zone and sustain casualties among his own troops for ground he would have to turn over to the Russians at the end of the war.

Since the Combined Chiefs of Staff gave him no specific instructions to

take Berlin, Eisenhower proceeded along the lines he had already laid down.

With the Ruhr encircled on 2nd April, Eisenhower sent Montgomery to the Elbe River, Bradley to the line of the Elbe and Mulde Rivers, and Devers to Nuremberg, then beyond to Linz, Austria.

Allied troops reached the Elbe River on 11th April. Although the US Ninth Army was then fifty miles from Berlin, and although the army commander, William Simpson, believed that he could get there, Eisenhower said there would be no further advance to the east. The Russians by then were bestirring themselves to move the few remaining miles into the city.

On 30th April, Hitler committed suicide, and the Russians took Berlin.

For all practical purposes, that ended the war in Europe. On the morning of 7th May, when German military authorities signed a formal document of unconditional surrender, Eisenhower cabled the Combined Chiefs: 'The mission of this Allied force was fulfilled'.

Shortly thereafter, Marshall wrote to Eisenhower: 'You have completed your mission with the greatest victory in the history of warfare. You have commanded with outstanding success the most powerful military force that has ever been assembled. You have met and successfully disposed of every conceivable difficulty incident to varied national interests and international political problems of unprecedented complications . . . you have been selfless in your actions, always sound and tolerant in your

Field-Marshal Keitel signs the surrender documents in the Soviet Headquarters in Berlin ; standing at his left is Admiral Döenitz

judgments, and altogether admirable in the courage and wisdom of your military decisions.'

No finer tribute could have been extended.

Eisenhower had met and overcome a series of challenges that illuminated the great capacity of his leadership. He had mastered problems of incredible difficulty. He had shaped and preserved a coalition effort that had produced total victory. He brought credit and honor to all who served under his command and to all who participated in the triumphant struggle against the totalitarian tyranny of those years.

Summation

The Supreme Allied Commander

A surprising number of professional soldiers and military historians gave Eisenhower failing grades as a commander in the Second World War. They said he was hardly adequate as a wartime leader of troops.

The number of critics is surprising because of Eisenhower's immense popularity. Rarely has any American received the confidence and affection tendered to him as Supreme. Allied Commander.

What do they say against him?

He was lucky, his critics maintain, rather than expert. His greatest asset was a ready smile and a likeable personality that enabled him to win friends among influential men and admiration from the common people.

He lacked battle experience, his detractors claim. He never heard a shot fired in anger. He never commanded a unit in combat, except, of course, all the forces in the European theater of operations, and there he was blessed with splendid subordinates: Bedell Smith as his chief of staff to run his Allied Force Headquarters in the Mediterranean and later his Supreme Headquarters in Europe; Alexander, Bradley, Tedder, Montgomery, Spaatz, Devers, Cunningham, Patton, and others to conduct the fighting.

His job as Supreme Allied Commander permitted him to act like a chairman of the board who presided over deliberations and directed a vast enterprise by remote control. He hated to make decisions, hesitated to take action on the battlefield, disliked interfering with his combat leaders.

He was, they tell us, no more than a glorified message center between Washington and the field, keeping his immediate superiors, Marshall and the Combined Chiefs of Staff, informed of developments and transmitting their instructions to his subordinates.

His function was primarily ceremonial. His most effective performance was to visit troop units in the interest of sustaining and bolstering morale.

His reputation thus rests, they argue, on certain non-military qualities. Photogenic, amiable, and easy to get along with, Eisenhower was supreme commander, they say, because he had no firm military convictions, was amenable to suggestion, and would bring little harm to projects determined by his superiors and executed by his subordinates.

This portrait emerges in private conversations and discussions among retired generals and in casual exchanges of ideas among military historians.

For example, a retired general tells this story of what he considers to be a typical illustration of Eisenhower's inability to make up his mind. An infantry division embarking for invasion was already aboard its ships when an air force officer, over the protests of navy and army officers, insisted on adding to the over-crowded vessels a cargo of aerial bombs. Since this would require unloading some of the ground force equipment regarded as essential for the landings, representatives of the three services went to Eisenhower for a resolution of the problem.

Unwilling to rule, Eisenhower sent the three officers to another room with instructions to return in five minutes with a recommended solution. In the adjoining room, the air force representative was quick to realize he was outnumbered two to one. This was the decision reported to Eisenhower, who accepted it.

A judgment worthy of Solomon? Not at all, the narrator says. On the contrary, Eisenhower's behavior was unmilitary, for he was reluctant to make a decision, and making decisions is what generals are paid for.

One of the most unflattering characterizations of Eisenhower appeared in print in 1946, a year after the end of the Second World War, in Ralph Ingersoll's book *Top Secret*. According to Ingersoll, Eisenhower was a pawn of the British, a front-office stooge, a yes-man who took credit for the

Eisenhower hears of atrocities committed by concentration camp staff

battles won by his subordinates.

'By nature a conciliator and an arbitrator,' Eisenhower 'had nothing whatever to do with leading the [Normandy] invasion,' Ingersoll writes. Instead, 'he backed up the powers of attorney he had given his three British Commanders-in-Chief' – Montgomery, Ramsay, and Leigh Mallory – while he remained 'almost wholly occupied in England with the statesman's part of the role of Supreme Commander. He visited the field forces for official inspections only.'

The sole purely military responsibility left to Eisenhower, according to Ingersoll, was his function as a go-between – keeping his three subordinate service commanders in touch with his own superiors, the Combined Chiefs of Staff. Though he bore the public responsibility, he did little more about the invasion than pace the floor and listen to the weather prophets who told him to proceed.

His headquarters, Ingersoll continues, was designed to coordinate the Anglo-American war effort rather than to command actively in the field and to win battles; to be informed of decisions – on strategy by the Combined Chiefs and the heads of the two Allied states, and on tactics by his field commanders – instead of making decisions.

In sum, Ingersoll argues, Eisenhower left the actual management of the war to those with more experience. Instead of maintaining a strong hand at the helm, Eisenhower was nothing more than 'a chairman – a shrewd, intelligent, tactful chairman' – who had been 'especially selected for his ability to conciliate, to see both points of view, to be above national interests – and to be neither bold nor decisive, and neither a leader nor a general.'

In short, Eisenhower failed to coincide with Ingersoll's conception of a military leader.

Eleven years later, in 1957, Arthur

Bryant wrote a history of the war, *The Turn of the Tide*. It is an excellent account with a pronounced British point of view, for the book is based on the diaries of Brooke, Marshall's counterpart who became Field Marshal Lord Alanbrooke, Chief of the Imperial General Staff. Alanbrooke's view was much like Ingersoll's.

'Eisenhower,' Alanbrooke says, 'had never even commanded a battalion in action when he found himself commanding a group of Armies in North Africa. No wonder he was at a loss as to what to do, and allowed himself to be absorbed in the political situation at the expense of the tactical. I had little confidence in his having the ability to handle the military situation confronting him, and he caused me great anxiety . . . He learnt a lot during the war, but tactics, strategy and command were never his strong points.'

At the Casablanca Conference in January, 1943, when the Combined Chiefs decided to unify the North African theater under Eisenhower's command, Alanbrooke recorded his private thoughts as follows: Eisenhower 'had neither the tactical nor strategical experience required for such a task. By bringing Alexander over from the Middle East and appointing him as Deputy to Eisenhower, we were . . . flattering and pleasing the Americans in so far as we were placing our senior and experienced commander to function under their commander who had no war experience. . . We were pushing Eisenhower up into the stratosphere and rarefied atmosphere of a Supreme Commander, where he would be free to devote his time to the political and inter-allied problems, whilst we inserted under him one of our own commanders to deal with the military situations and to restore the necessary drive and coordination which had been so seriously lacking.'

'Where he shone,' Alanbrooke writes, 'was his ability to handle Allied forces, to treat them all with strict impartiality, and to get the very best out of an inter-Allied force . . . he was uncommonly well served by his Chief of Staff, Bedell Smith, who had far more flair for military matters than his master. In addition Ike was blest with a wonderful charm that carried him far; perhaps his greatest asset was a greater share of luck than most of us receive in life. However, if Ike had rather more than his share of luck we, as allies, were certainly extremely fortunate to have such an exceptionally charming individual. As Supreme Commander what he may have lacked in military ability he greatly made up for by the charm of his personality.'

Alanbrooke's judgment is surely an acidulous and back handed compliment.

A more recent book to attempt to measure generalship is Colonel Trevor N Dupuy's *Combat Leaders of World War II*, published in 1965. Dupuy concisely sums up the case against Eisenhower without accepting it entirely. 'Eisenhower's detractors,' Dupuy writes, 'claim that he had no real combat command experience and was merely a genial "chairman of the board"; a political general who could get along well with the British and who leaned over backward to avoid interallied and interservice controversies; a man who preferred to settle disputes and to solve problems by compromise rather than by decision; a soldier who failed to understand the basic strategical issues involved in the defeat of Germany. He has been criticized by his subordinates Montgomery, Bradley, and Patton, not only for having failed to make a strategic decision for a truly decisive main effort in Western Europe but also for hesitancy in carrying out the more cautious decisions which he did make.'

Given Eisenhower's extreme popularity both during and after the war, how explain such caustic characterizations of one of the greatest heroes of the Second World War? Jealousy? Politics? Or something more sub-

stantial?

Jealousy there doubtless was. Eisenhower was outranked by many of his subordinates. Promoted over a host of officers who were senior to him on the rolls of the regular army, Eisenhower had the difficult task of asserting his primacy over those who remembered him as a rather junior officer during the pre-Second World War period. At least one of his division commanders was a brigadier-general when young Major Eisenhower and his wife came to call.

Some contend that Marshall sent Eisenhower to England in 1942 in order to hold the command of the cross-Channel invasion for Marshall himself. The events between June 1942, when Eisenhower arrived in England, and June 1944, when the Allies crossed the Channel, demonstrated clearly Eisenhower's capacity to command the complicated aspects of what was probably the most complex military operation in history. If he was, indeed, sent to hold the fort for Marshall, he soon outgrew the role, for his quickly increasing maturity made him no-one's man but his own.

Was politics responsible for some of the castigation of his wartime performance? Undoubtedly it was, and particularly after his entry into domestic politics. Operating in the unfamiliar field of national politics in the 1950s, Eisenhower could put his foot into his mouth with incredible ease. His befuddled sentences muddled by foggy logic became classic. His critics assumed that his military utterances had been much like his Presidential pronouncements.

What they failed to realize was his mastery of the military area. At a briefing for a group of VIPs in Paris while he was commanding SHAPE in the early 1950s, Eisenhower spontane-

ously took the pointer and made the presentation himself. At the end of his extemporaneous talk, his audience of hard-headed politicians and business men stood and cheered – literally. They were impressed by his grasp of realities and his translation of them into comprehensible English and dazzled by the clarity and force of his expression. He was at home in the military field.

Does something more substantial explain the criticism of his role as the Supreme Allied Commander? His critics point to several crises during the Mediterranean and European campaigns where he manifested less than a crystal clear direction of events.

For example, what about the inability of the Allied troops to seize Tunisia before the arrival of Axis forces later in 1942? What of his failure to close the Argentan-Falaise pocket firmly in August 1944? How about the debate in the fall of 1944 between those who advocated a broad-front strategy and those who wished to concentrate the Allied resources for an exploitation on a narrow front? And Berlin – would not a great military figure have grasped the strategic significance of the German capital and have driven vigorously to capture it instead of being diverted uselessly in quest of what turned out to be a phantom German National Redoubt?

These are the most serious issues, the salient points in the indictment that Eisenhower was less than adequate as a military commander. How valid is the charge?

The years that have passed since the end of the Second World War are surely enough time to make possible a dispassionate examination of the case for and against Eisenhower as a soldier.

In this connection, two questions are worth considering. Can the charges levelled by his critics be supported? And how does he rate and rank with other great American figures of military history?

Answering these questions is as

Anthony Eden, British Foreign Secretary, is greeted by Eisenhower on the occasion of the former's visit to Normandy in August 1944

The Class of 1915, United States
Military Academy. Eisenhower is in
the third row from the front, right of
center

Walter Krueger was impressed by Eisenhower's abilities when he was Krueger's Third Army Chief of Staff

Patton, without question one of the great combat leaders of all time, was serious when he codenamed his Third Army headquarters LUCKY. In accordance with the code used on the telephone or over the radio, as the Army Commander he was known as LUCKY 6. Was he superstitious? He was an avid student of military history, and he appreciated the importance of luck as an ingredient of success.

Eisenhower's decision for D-Day discloses the marvellous good fortune he enjoyed. The date for the invasion of north-west Europe having been set, the incredibly complicated machinery for launching the greatest amphibious operation of the war having gotten under way, everything was in readiness for the attack when the weather on which the whole operation depended turned bad. Worsening weather would bring disaster to the climactic blow on which the Allies had staked their chances of winning the war in the near future.

Should the invasion go, or should it be postponed? After a delay of one day, the weather still looked threatening, but Eisenhower decided to go. Intuition, foolhardiness, or luck, it was the correct decision. The invasion went as scheduled, all the better for the poor weather because the Germans on the other side of the Channel doubted that any man would have the nerve to launch an invasion at that time in those conditions.

Was Eisenhower a military expert? Look at his professional background. He absorbed and profited from all the schooling the army had to offer. For six years, between 1929 and 1935, he served at the top level of the army – in the offices of the Assistant Secretary of War and of the Chief of Staff. He commanded tank battalions in the 1920s, served at regimental level, then held posts successively at division, corps, and army echelons – all before the United States entered the Second World War.

His promotions during the First and

difficult as measuring quality. Emotion enters the process of judgment, colors evaluation, and renders conclusions a matter of opinion.

Disregarding the honors that came to him after the Second World War, let us consider his merit as a military commander. Was he, as is sometimes alleged, not really very good? Or will the reputation he acquired and enjoyed during the war remain one of his enduring claims to fame?

Let us take the charges one by one and analyze their substance and relevance.

Was he lucky? He certainly was. All great leaders in any field of endeavor have luck. Without that intangible good fortune of having things come out right in the end, all the expertise in the world goes for naught.

It is better to be lucky than wise; an ounce of luck is better than a pound of wisdom – are only two of many sayings that illustrate what has long been observed, that luck is an indispensable asset of those who succeed.

Second World Wars amply argue his case as an expert, for his rise in rank during both was exceedingly rapid, even for a West Pointer. In 1915 he was a second lieutenant; three years later a lieutenant-colonel, the second man in his class of 164 West Point graduates to reach that rank. In 1941 he was a lieutenant-colonel; three years later he had five-star rank.

To say that these promotions were based on a smile and an engaging personality is an affront to a system that is ruthless in preventing the inefficient from reaching and remaining in places of great responsibility. Despite claims by the disgruntled, the non-expert has little chance to advance to high rank in the army.

Was he blessed with the ability to impress influential people? Absolutely yes. For almost five years, from 1935 to 1940, he was MacArthur's assistant in the Philippines. MacArthur was not notably tolerant of the inefficient.

In June 1941, Eisenhower was Walter Krueger's Third Army Chief of Staff. Krueger too was a hard-boiled old pro, and he recognized Eisenhower's abilities and helped push him up the ladder of rank to greater responsibility.

In early 1942, as Chief of the War Plans Division of the War Department General Staff, then as Chief of the Operations Division in the Chief of Staff's office, Eisenhower impressed Marshall sufficiently with his capacity to win appointment in June of that year as commanding general of the European theater.

One can be sure that MacArthur, Krueger, and Marshall were hardly taken in by a pleasant smile, a likeable personality, or soft-soap. To have impressed these generals is a recommendation of the highest kind.

What did impress them? Mentally quick and bright, Eisenhower had a capacity for learning, an ability for assessing complicated situations, a facility for striking to the heart of a problem. He usually came up unerringly with the right solution. In

Marshall shared Eisenhower's ability to choose the best and most loyal advisers and subordinates

sum, his judgment was sound, his balance excellent.

Add an ability to get along with people and the result is a rare person – sharp, smart, and persuasive, one fitted by intelligence and temperament for high command and for the association with officials of high rank that responsibility demands.

What of Eisenhower's battle experience? He never commanded a small unit in action. Except for the sound of artillery and air bombardment, except for the distant chatter of machine guns or a far-off fusillade of musketry, he probably never heard a shot fired in anger.

Whether this disqualifies a soldier from holding high command is a moot question. It is interesting to note that Bradley first exercised command in combat at the corps level, a rather high place to break into the occupation of combat leader. Yet this hardly hindered him from becoming recognized as probably the most brilliant practitioner of grand tactics

His talent for bringing out the best in his commanders was his most valuable asset

in the European theater. Marshall, the strategic architect of the Second World War, who more than any other was responsible for the overall direction of the war, never had a field command in wartime.

In some respects Eisenhower was much like Marshall. He had an intuitive ability to surround himself with capable advisers and subordinates. And he was able to call upon them and receive from them the utmost in loyalty and effort.

Twice during the war Patton's indiscretions brought him close to dismissal: the slapping incidents in Sicily and a security breach in England before the cross-Channel invasion. Although a lesser man would have fired Patton, Eisenhower gave him a severe tongue-lashing and kept

him. Appreciating Patton's combat leadership, he was convinced that American troops would win more rapidly with Patton in the field.

Bedell Smith, his chief of staff, exemplified Eisenhower's happy facility for having the right man in the right job. Eisenhower without Smith, his critics aver, would have been lost. But Smith did what Eisenhower wanted. He frequently acted as Eisenhower's hatchet man and performed some of the unpleasant duties that are an unavoidable part of command. No one has ever questioned who was boss.

But, some would say, it was really Marshall who sent Smith over to keep Eisenhower on the straight and narrow. Smith was Marshall's man. If this was so at the beginning, Smith soon lost any split allegiance he might have had. During the negotiations for the surrender of Italy in the summer of 1943, Smith, who played an important role in the military diplomacy, carried out Eisenhower's wishes, not Marshall's which were in some discord with the policy that Eisenhower enunciated and executed. According to Alanbrooke, 'Eisenhower wanted to offer the Italians an easy and honourable way out . . . in return for immediate use of their airfields and strategic strongpoints' - and he had his way over the objections of the politicians and strategists in Washington and London.

Was Smith particularly useful because Eisenhower was unable to be tough? It seems more likely that Eisenhower rarely chose to play that rôle. Yet he could, when he had to, be ruthless, firm, and resolute. Montgomery, who wanted desperately to be the ground forces commander in north-west Europe, harassed Eisenhower through most of the campaign. Eisenhower was extremely patient and finally put him in his place. At the end of the war, Montgomery's tribute to his commander, recorded in his book *Normandy to the Baltic* is somewhat touching and even slightly pathetic.

Nor did Eisenhower hesitate when it came to weeding out inefficient officers. Some thought him rather heartless. One corps commander in North Africa and two in southern Italy got the axe - to say nothing of the division commanders who were relieved.

The Eisenhower temper was one of the better-kept secrets of the war. But many associates testify to the astringent and explosive - almost choleric - reaction he had to evidence of ineffectiveness. The men he selected usually worked out well. Those who were sent to him were the ones who were more apt to perform beneath his expectations and standards.

Eisenhower's brilliance in selecting and working with his American colleagues was matched by his success with the British. Assisted in the Mediterranean by Alexander, Cunningham, and Tedder - who commanded, respectively, the Allied ground, sea, and air forces - Eisenhower welded them, as well as his Anglo-American staff, into a well-balanced team. It was the same in north-west Europe. 'Thanks to Eisenhower,' even Alanbrooke had to concede, 'there was remarkably little friction' between the officers of the two nations.

Commanding a coalition effort, Eisenhower - and perhaps only he could have done it so smoothly and with such flair - made it work. He did it so naturally that American purists called him pro-British, while British extremists accused him of being pro-American. In one instance, when certain influential British officers urged him vainly to get rid of Montgomery, they charged Eisenhower with being too British. What they failed to recognize was his ability to combine skillfully the best characteristics and procedures of both nations.

Some Americans think he gave up certain prerogatives of command because he conducted the war in the British fashion of commanding by committee. To the degree that he accommodated himself to this British practice he showed not weakness but rather flexibility. He consulted his subordinate commanders more than Americans are apt to, he called frequent conferences, he asked often for expressions of opinion. Without these amenities, it is doubtful that he would have secured, at least at first, the cooperation and ultimately the devotion of his non-American associates.

It is significant that he maintained his relative independence and freedom as theater commander. His rejection of interference by higher authority was an American rather than a British characteristic. The British on occasion sought to exert over him the close supervision they normally exercised over British theater commanders. He resisted gracefully. Despite Churchill's enormous pressure, for example, to call off the invasion of southern France, Eisenhower was convinced that the landings

**On more than one occasion
Eisenhower tactfully stood out against
Churchill's pressing demands**

were necessary, and he brought them off. There was never any question who the Supreme Allied Commander was in the Mediterranean and in northwest Europe.

It is interesting that Churchill's insistence on and his eventual engineering of the Anzio invasion occurred at the time when Eisenhower was departing the Mediterranean theater to assume command of the OVERLORD forces in England. Had Eisenhower remained in the Mediterranean, it is possible that Churchill might have been unable to bulldoze aside the objections of the professional soldiers who advised against the Anzio landings, landings that failed to achieve their purpose, the immediate capture of Rome.

Even Alanbrooke acknowledged on at least two occasions 'the moral courage' of Eisenhower and on a third occasion his 'good sense'. To name

another instance of Eisenhower's brilliance, Alanbrooke characterized his handling of Darlan and his military agreement with the French in North Africa as a master stroke for which Eisenhower 'took full responsibility' and deserved it. 'Eisenhower never flinched,' Alanbrooke noted; his 'firmness was rewarded.'

Was Eisenhower in constant contact with his superiors in Washington and in London? Of course. Many messages, quite a few of them personal communications for 'Marshall's eyes only'. flashed from his headquarters, and a great many were received. Marshall often asked for recommendations, explanations, and clarifications, frequently offered guidance and advice, but never told Eisenhower what to do. Most of Eisenhower's messages to his chief were informative in purpose, nature, and content. In a war of global proportions, all parts of the whole had to fit into the overall concept and plan. Since the Combined Chiefs set objectives and allocated resources, they had to remain in closest touch with the commanders who ran the theaters of war.

What of the substantive issues? How about Eisenhower's inability to thrust eastward from Algiers to Bizerte and Tunis in November and December of 1942 before the Axis forces managed to build up a formidable opposition? The eastward thrust from Algiers came to an unhappy end as a consequence of the onset of the rainy season and the inability of the slender Allied logistical system to support a prolonged drive. Calling off the offensive was an unpleasant decision – as Alanbrooke noted with admiration of Eisenhower's fortitude – but Eisenhower faced up directly to the stalemate that had developed. A lesser man might have persisted, and the only result would have been a higher Allied casualty rate.

To what extent was he to blame for the unhappy experience at Kasserine Pass? There is no doubt that Eisenhower misjudged the capacity of Fredendall, whom Marshall had recommended as a commander. Having finally recognized Fredendall's shortcomings, Eisenhower tolerated them too long.

This, of course, is clearer in retrospect. The only extenuation of Eisenhower's hesitancy to remove Fredendall lies in Eisenhower's relative inexperience at the head of the supreme command. Still learning how to function in that place of high responsibility, Eisenhower probably lacked the self-confidence that he gained increasingly as the war continued.

His reluctance to relieve Fredendall stemmed from his unwillingness to hurt Marshall, who had selected Fredendall in the first place, his fear of disrupting the alliance, his concern over whom he could find to replace Fredendall, and his feeling that Fredendall would learn his trade as a combat leader and adapt to the realities.

When Eisenhower was satisfied that Fredendall would not do, he waited until the end of the battle to relieve him – probably because of innate courtesy and also because he had already sent Harmon forward to help.

The reforms that subsequently shook down the Americans and made them combat worthy were inspired by Eisenhower although carried out by Patton.

Was Eisenhower to blame for permitting the escape from Normandy of two German field armies that were virtually, but not quite, surrounded at Argentan and Falaise? There is some justification for feeling that Eisenhower let events slip out of his control, through his fingers. Montgomery was then, in August 1944, the ground forces commander, and though Bradley encircled the German troops who had pushed into Mortain, Montgomery's failure to remove the army group boundary halted Bradley at the edge of complete success.

Only Eisenhower could have intervened. Only Eisenhower could have ordered Montgomery to eliminate the restriction that held back the Americans. Eisenhower preferred to observe instead of interfering. He left the conduct of the battle to his subordinates.

Though he made no excuse, his reason for remaining aloof was the fact that his own headquarters was not yet established on the continent. He lacked the staff facilities – the intelligence, signal, and other information – that would have permitted him to reach a sound decision on a matter that required detailed and timely knowledge.

What of the broad-front, narrow-front controversy during the pursuit phase of the European operation, in the latter days of August, 1944 and the early days of September, when the Allied armies were streaming across the Seine and heading toward the Siegfried Line on the heels of the fleeing Germans? Should Eisenhower have allocated the bulk of his resources to one of the pursuing forces instead of spreading them among all?

The debate is usually discussed in strict military terms: mass, objective, and economy of force. These military issues were important, but the fundamental question was political and related to the proprieties of coalition warfare. Eisenhower had many obligations – to his troops of various nations, to those directing the war, and to the British and American publics.

How could he slight a British commander in favor of an American, or vice-versa? The stability of the coalition rested on delicate conditions, and the broad-front strategy, a compromise adopted by Eisenhower over Montgomery's vehement protests and Bradley's quiet reservations, fulfilled the conditions for equilibrium better than any other course of action. No-one received favored treatment.

'Eisenhower', Bryant writes, giving Alanbrooke's thoughts in quite another context that has relevance to this situation, 'might be without experience of war but he had precisely the qualities – of character, selflessness and good sense – to knit the staff officers of two nations into an integrated organization in which national differences and jealousies were forgotten. His insistence that Anglo-American rivalry was the unforgivable sin created in his raw headquarters a new conception of inter-Allied unity.'

'Alliances in the past,' Eisenhower once wrote, 'have often done no more than to name the common foe, and "unity of command" has been a pious aspiration thinly disguising the national jealousies, ambitions and recriminations of high-ranking officers, unwilling to subordinate themselves or their forces to a commander of different nationality or different service.'

This was hardly the case where Eisenhower himself directed. In his case, the different strategic and doctrinal concepts of British and Americans were not allowed to dislocate the single-minded pursuit of victory.

Divergent opinions on the best way to attain that goal were resolved by Eisenhower in such a way that no residue of ill-feeling disrupted the performance of the entire military machine.

Even the attempts of Montgomery, supported by Brooke and to a lesser extent by Churchill, to assume the Allied ground command, attempts that persisted long beyond justification, were countered by Eisenhower's firmness that preserved the smooth workings of the coalition war.

As for the question of who was correct, Eisenhower in espousing the broad-front strategy or Montgomery in calling for a single thrust on a narrow front, the compelling element was the ability of the logistical system to support the Allied drive. More clearly than any of his subordinates, Eisenhower appreciated that the great and unexpected speed of the advance across France had outstripped the capacity of the logistical organization to serve the combat units.

Montgomery claimed he could drive all the way to Berlin, and Patton bemoaned the lack of gasoline that prevented him from cutting the Germans to ribbons. But Eisenhower knew – perhaps intuitively – that the logistical apparatus established in Normandy and expanding slowly behind the combat units was unable to support even a single, concentrated thrust in the decisive strength required to bring the Germans to their knees in the latter months of 1944. This has become crystal clear in historical perspective.

The failure to take Berlin? Berlin was simply not on the cards. Given the political guidance Eisenhower received from the Combined Chiefs, given the strict military aims enunciated by the Anglo-American alliance, and given the constitutional principle in both nations of civilian supremacy and control over the military, it was impossible for Eisenhower or anyone else in his position to go beyond the Elbe River. The partici-

pants who work within the confines of a policy structure framed within the context of a particular time period are, unfortunately, deprived of the clarity that is the undisputed possession of the Monday-morning quarterback.

Much more important is the fact that the Russians could have taken Berlin as early as February 1945. Though Berlin was at most a week's drive away, the Russians chose to procrastinate while their armies moved forward on other fronts. They were reluctant to deliver the *coup de grace*, dispatch the crumbling Nazi structure into oblivion, and finish off the war until they had overrun eastern Europe. Had the Allied forces made a move toward Berlin, there is little doubt that the Russians could have reached the city first nonetheless.

The fact is that Eisenhower's superb accomplishment in the Second World War was his management of the complex establishment that won the war in north-western Europe.

Eisenhower with Soviet representatives after the signing of Germany's surrender

If his function resembled on occasion that of a chairman of the board, it was because the warfare of his time and place required it. In addition to his responsibility for winning battles, Eisenhower had duties that were, from a narrow and old-fashioned point of view, somewhat non-military. He was concerned – and he had to be – with civilian relations, fiscal policy in liberated countries, political problems, and what might be called military diplomacy – how to deal with the French in North Africa, how to negotiate the surrender of Italy, how to regard the status of the Free French during the liberation of France. If he interfered little with the tactical decisions of his subordinate commanders, it was because he was sometimes too busy with other matters and, more frequently, because he had complete confidence in their abilities.

Yet he had no hesitation in settling disagreements on the tactical level. Pantelleria fell easily to Allied troops because Eisenhower, over the arguments of subordinates, insisted it could be softened by air and naval bombardment. Over the protests of Leigh Mallory, he ordered the airborne drops in Normandy. He showed no reluctance in changing the entire plan and course of the Normandy campaign in the early days of August, when he swung the bulk of his forces eastward toward the Seine and away from Brittany.

He faltered not one iota in deciding to cross the Seine instead of pausing there in accordance with all prior planning. He had no hesitation in capping the unexpected capture of the Remagen bridge by pushing immediate exploitation of that event and building up forces on the east bank of the Rhine. During the Bulge, over the objections of some of his closest advisers, he placed Montgomery in command of American troops on the northern shoulder in order to fulfill the precept of unity of command.

There are many instances of his direct personal influence on the battlefield.

More often than not, Eisenhower's decisions reflected a compromise. The very nature of his command position, as well as the strength and closeness of the coalition, required tact and discretion. Whereas MacArthur in the South Pacific could run the show in a rather high-handed manner because the Americans were contributing the overwhelmingly preponderant strength in that theater, the case was different in Europe. British strength exceeded American commitments in the early part of the war, and not until the final year of the struggle did the American resources pull ahead.

Perhaps more to the point, Eisenhower exercised the supreme Allied command in the tradition of Ferdinand Foch. Placed in overall command of the Allied forces in the First World War – British, French, American, and eventually Italian — for the last seven months of the war, Foch lacked some of the normal prerogatives of command. He was, for example, unable to coerce the leaders of the national contingents into obeying his orders if it meant acting against their will. Their cooperation with him and with each other depended on Foch's powers of persuasion.

Foch walked and talked softly, trying always, and usually succeeding, to convince the national military commanders to follow courses of action that led to the common goal of common victory.

Supreme Allied command was new in the early years of the 20th Century, and it came about late in the First World War. It took the serious reverses brought about by Ludendorff's spring offensive in 1918 – which, like the Ardennes counteroffensive in 1944, was a final, all-out effort on the part of the Germans to win – to compel the Allies to act in concert. Because of their reluctance to submit their armies to the full range of command wielded by an officer of another nationality, Foch as Supreme Allied Commander functioned in large part as a coordinator.

So did Eisenhower a quarter of a century later. The important difference is that what Foch established, Eisenhower extended. As Supreme Allied Commander in the Second World War, Eisenhower was more than a coordinator and he received more than cooperation. Although he lacked the full extent of command authority over his British colleagues that he enjoyed over his American associates, he commanded and directed, supremely, and he was obeyed.

Part of Eisenhower's great strength as a commander lay precisely in his popularity. There was a quality of humanness about him that stemmed from his directness and simplicity. Much like President Truman, who gained sympathy by his humility when he was forced to step into the shoes of a giant, Eisenhower had the common touch that brought understanding. He imparted the impression that he was an ordinary human being doing the very best he could in a situation fraught with danger and difficulty.

He leveled with the press, took news correspondents into his confidence, and made it clear always that he was responsible for whatever might or did go wrong. During the few hours before the D-day invasion, he scribbled a note taking full responsibility in the event that the landings failed. In the Bulge, he insisted that he had been wrong to be so surprised by the German attack.

He had no need to assert his responsibility for what went right, for the people of the Allied nations stood solidly behind him.

In his 'rapid grooming for high office,' Chester Wilmot wrote in 1952 in his *The Struggle for Europe*, 'there was not time for Eisenhower to go through the mill of command and gain battle experience. On the other hand, the ten years in Washington and Manila had given him intimate knowledge of politico-military problems at the highest level and a breadth of outlook unusual in a regular soldier. This training stood him in good stead when he rose to be Commander-in-Chief for Operation TORCH. In this post the personal and political integrity of the man was more important than the professional ability of the soldier. Others could – and did – provide expert and experienced leadership in the field, but nobody else revealed Eisenhower's remarkable capacity for integrating the efforts of different allies and rival services and for creating harmony between individuals with varied backgrounds and temperaments. From the outset he demanded "immediate and continuous loyalty to the concept of unity" . . . Because he remained true to this principle, Eisenhower was to become the most successful commander of Allied forces in the history of war.'

Are any predecessors and contemporaries comparable with Eisenhower? Pershing comes to mind despite real differences in the circumstances. Pershing commanded only American troops in Europe. And the imperfect state of communications, making close touch between France and Washington impossible, required virtually complete independence of action on Pershing's part.

But probably the most important difference was the rôle of the United States in world affairs. In 1917, Britain and France were the leaders. The United States had yet to prove its strength, its military know-how. Convinced that the inexperienced American troops would perform better under French and British leadership, the Allied nations wanted to use them to stiffen existing formations along the front. Under instructions to retain the national identity of the American commitment, Pershing had to be tough and uncompromising. On the defensive until American units proved their combat worth near the end of the war, Pershing might be likened to the exponent of the 'hard sell'.

In the 1940s, America was the leader of the Allied coalition, and Eisenhower's appointment as supreme commander symbolized the status. Eisenhower could be, and was, affable, amiable, relaxed, the exponent of the soft sell.

MacArthur? When war came to the United States in 1941, MacArthur had already made his mark. He had a brilliant First World War record, and he had reached the pinnacle of advancement as US Army Chief of Staff. A distinguished figure, he commanded his theater during the Second World War in what now seems like splendid aloofness.

Marshall suggested that MacArthur organize a coalition theater command structure along the lines established by Eisenhower. But MacArthur retained a staff that was completely American.

Perhaps MacArthur was not as

flexible as Eisenhower. In a sense, MacArthur represented an earlier tradition, the heritage of Pershing. Eisenhower inaugurated a broader framework of operations more in tune with the nature of coalition warfare in the middle years of the century.

What if MacArthur had commanded the European theater? Would he have been so successful? Would he have been able immediately to impress the British to such an extent as to gain an entirely free hand in running the show alone?

It seems doubtful. The British had too much at stake.

Would MacArthur, if faced with the necessity of doing so, have been able to create and make work a close coalition effort like Eisenhower's? This too seems doubtful. During the Korean War, MacArthur had a unique opportunity to create a real United Nations command. By a brilliant stroke he could have organized a headquarters symbolizing the Free World's aspirations. Instead, he maintained the traditional American organization, no different from that of the First World War, no different from his own Second World War experience. He might have established on the military plane, somewhat in the manner of Eisenhower's postwar Supreme Headquarters, Allied Powers Europe (SHAPE), the leadership of the United States in a Pacific coalition of Free World nations.

Younger in outlook, a figure firmly rooted in his own times, Eisenhower maintained the ascendancy of American arms with an unparalleled ease and graciousness. Not only did he make a complex coalition work superbly, but he also remained a heroic figure to the troops of all the Allied nations under his command.

Not a Patton, a Bradley, or a Montgomery, Eisenhower directed them and engineered victory in Europe. In so doing, he became a hero worthy of praise and adulation.

According to Alfred F Hurley, as a man, Eisenhower remained 'unspoiled

by his many triumphs.' He was 'faithful to his Kansas heritage.' He was 'completely dedicated to his profession and to the cause for which the Allies fought.'

As a general, he was 'more than a politician in uniform, which is all that some critics would concede to him.' Yet 'he was adept in his relations with his superiors and in his handling of

politically sensitive situations.'

As a leader, he was 'pugnacious in the prosecution of his part of the war; perceptive in his understanding of the rôles of land, sea, and air forces in combined warfare; unshaken during and after rare setbacks; tough-minded.'

America's greatest field commander in the Second World War, Eisenhower

18th June 1945. Crowds line Washington's Constitution Avenue to welcome Eisenhower on his return from Europe

represented more than anyone else the new leadership and the new American rôle in world history. His achievement was great. His military stature is assured.

Bibliography

The Supreme Commander: The War Years of General Dwight D Eisenhower Stephen E Ambrose
The Duel for France Martin Blumenson
A Soldier's Story Omar N Bradley
The Turn of the Tide: Study based on the Diaries and Autobiographical Notes of Field Marshal the Viscount Alanbrooke Sir Arthur Bryant
My Three Years with Eisenhower Captain Harry C Butcher
Crusade for Europe Dwight D Eisenhower
The Mighty Endeavor Charles B MacDonald
Normandy to the Baltic Field Marshal Sir Bernard L Montgomery
The Supreme Command Forrest C Pogue
The Struggle for Europe Chester Wilmot
NOTE: I am indebted for permission to use my article 'Eisenhower', from *Army* Magazine, June 1966. Copyright 1966 by Association of the U.S. Army